HARRY WINSTON
The Ultimate Jeweler

HARRY WINSTON

The Ultimate Jeweler

BY LAURENCE S. KRASHES

RONALD WINSTON, EDITOR

FRONTISPIECE: HARRY WINSTON, 1896–1978. © ALFRED EISENSTAEDT

*Published in New York, New York, and
Santa Monica, California, by Harry Winston, Inc.
and the Gemological Institute of America*

Copyright © 1986 by Ronald Winston

*All rights reserved. No part of this book may be used,
reproduced, or transmitted by any means, electronic or mechanical,
including photocopying, recording, or by any retrieval system,
without the written permission of the publishers.*

*First Edition—1984
Second Edition, Revised—1986*

*ISBN 0-87311-015-3
Library of Congress Catalog Number: 84-51658*

Manufactured in Japan

CONTENTS

ix	FOREWORD
x	ACKNOWLEDGMENTS
xii	INTRODUCTION
1	NO STONE UNTURNED: THE STORY OF HARRY WINSTON
37	AN EMPIRE BUILT ON DIAMONDS

46	ARCOTS	102	NEPAL
50	ANASTASIA	104	NIARCHOS
51	ASHOKA	106	NUR-UL-AIN TIARA
52	BRIOLETTE	108	OPPENHEIMER
54	CORNFLOWER BLUE	109	POHL
55	CROWN OF CHARLEMAGNE	110	PORTUGUESE
56	COUNTESS SZÉCHÉNYI	112	PORTER RHODES
60	DEEPDENE	113	QAMAR-I-SALTANA
62	DEAL SWEETENER	113	QUEEN OF GOLCONDA
63	EUGÉNIE BLUE	114	ROVENSKY
64	ÉTOILE DU DÉSERT	115	SHAH OF PERSIA
66	HOPE	116	SHAKESPEARE MARQUISE
79	IDOL'S EYE	117	STAR OF THE EAST
81	INDORE PEAR SHAPES	121	STAR OF SIERRA LEONE
84	JONKER	122	STAR OF INDEPENDENCE
88	KING GEORGE IV	124	STAR OF THE SOUTH
91	LAL QILA	125	STAR OF SULEIMAN
92	LESOTHO	125	STONEWINS
93	LIBERATOR	126	TAYLOR-BURTON
94	LOUIS XIV	128	TITAN OVAL
96	MABEL BOLL	129	VARGAS
98	McFARLIN	132	WASHINGTON
99	NASSAK	133	WINSTON
100	NAPOLEON NECKLACE	135	WINSTON HEART SHAPE

137	AN EMPIRE BUILT ON JEWELRY
211	APPENDIX
212	NOTES
214	BIBLIOGRAPHY

O KING, as the diamond is pure throughout, so, O King, should the sincere man of virtue, constant in the right endeavour, be ever pure in his manner of living. This, O King, is the first quality of the diamond he ought to have. Again, O King, as the diamond cannot be alloyed with inferior substance, so, O King, should the sincere man of virtue, constant in right endeavour, never mix in friendship with wicked men. This, O King, is the second quality of the diamond he ought to have. Again, O King, as the diamond is only set about with the most costly jewels, so, O King, should the sincere man of virtue, constant in the right endeavour, only associate with men of highest excellence. This, O King, is the third quality of the diamond he ought to have. For it was said, O King, by the Blessed One, Buddha:

> Let the pure mix only with the pure
> Ever in memory firm
> Dwelling in the harmony of wisdom
> Thus shall ye put an end to sorrow.

THE QUESTIONING OF KING MELINDA

FOREWORD

Harry Winston led an exemplary life, rich in legend, lore, and mystery. It was a life fantastic that he enjoyed to its fullest extent, weaving a fable of his own world, one filled with stories of kings and maharajas and great jewels and fortunes made and lost. He lived out the dream of being famous and successful in a place and time where it was all possible and in a field which had never before and probably never again will witness such a creative genius.

Sometimes when the burden of being personality and fabulist one and the same seemed too great, and the weight of the world became too much, he would bemoan to himself with a sense of humor and self-mockery so characteristic of him, "Oh, Harry, Harry darling," he would say with a sigh.

It is to Harry, my father, that this book is dedicated, and to all the warm and wonderful memories that linger after him.

Ronald Winston

June, 1984

ACKNOWLEDGMENTS

To Ronald Winston for giving me the opportunity to create this tribute to his father, and for the help and encouragement he offered.

To Alice Keller, of the Gemological Institute of America, without whose expertise and patience this book would not have been completed. Both Mrs. Keller and her assistant, Sally Thomas, skillfully reworked the manuscript many times to put my thoughts into the well-written form herein. I made their job a nightmare and they always made mine a pleasure.

To A.V. Shinde, jewelry designer at Harry Winston since 1962 and one of the most talented designers in the world today. His incredibly precise and beautiful hand-painted renditions of jewelry pieces appear herein.

To Henry Ratz, who designed this splendid book, despite the formidable task of working with old, albeit unique, photos of these priceless pieces.

To Henry Baker, for his wonderful reminiscences of Harry Winston's early years in the New York jewelry trade and of his purchase of both the Stoddard and Huntington estates. At the age of 96, Mr. Baker is still very active in New York real estate.

For their valuable help in my research, I wish to thank the following people: Joseph Denton, New York City, for his ever-helpful counsel, advice, and sense of humor, without which I would be lost; Lawrence J. Fox, New York City, for reworking much of the original manuscript to help me find a better word or phrase; Hans Nadelhoffer, Geneva, Switzerland, for the work that he did to uncover the true story of the Briolette and the Eugénie Blue; James "Bob" Rose of Connoisseur Litho, New York City, for his recommendations and assistance in the restoration of many old photographs; David and Edward Weiss of Packaged Facts, New York City, whose research information firm was most accommodating; Trevor Hall, Hampshire, England, for verifying the information about royalty given herein; H.R.H. Prince R. Holkar, Indore, India; Countess Anthony Szapary, Newport, Rhode Island; Dr. Henry Meyer, Professor of Geology, Purdue University, West Lafayette, Indiana; Shirley Fairall, De Beers Public Relations, Johannesburg, South Africa; Elizabeth Dolan, Diamond Information Center, New York City; Sister Thomas Aquin, Albertus Magnus College, New Haven, Connecticut; and Grace Marcus of Harry Winston, who typed this manuscript so many times that she must have it memorized.

Laurence S. Krashes

ACKNOWLEDGMENTS TO SECOND EDITION

It is with heartfelt and gracious thanks that I once again acknowledge the magnificent job accomplished by Alice Keller, the project director, and Henry Ratz, the book designer. The worldwide acclaim and accolades that this book has received are due in no small way to their high degree of ability and professionalism.

My thanks go also to Cary Horowitz of Harry Winston, Inc., for the scholarly research he did on the Ahmedabad Diamond and the Star of the East.

LSK

INTRODUCTION

*He who buys a diamond
purchases a fragment of eternity.
She who wears a diamond
adorns herself with the pure rays
of Creation's dawn.*

FROM ANCIENT HINDU WRITINGS

The original intention of this book was to reproduce those entries in the Gemological Institute of America's *Diamond Dictionary* that involved diamonds handled by Harry Winston. While reviewing that material, however, I found so much additional information that the scope of the project changed dramatically. Many of the original GIA entries warranted updating, correction, or expansion. In addition, heretofore privileged information about many of the stones could now be released. Many articles about Harry Winston that had appeared in newspapers and magazines over the past six decades were resurrected, and numerous stories and anecdotes that had never appeared in print before were researched and verified. Furthermore, not only did Mr. Winston handle many major diamonds, but he also was responsible for stimulating the creation of some of the most highly prized jewelry in the world. Rarely had photographs and histories of these items been published. Here, then, was an opportunity to bring a great deal of fascinating information together in one book, thereby highlighting the life of Harry Winston as it was reflected in his career.

When Harry Winston examined a diamond, whether rough or polished, his genius enabled him to see possibilities others could never imagine. He was responsible for the cutting of such famous diamonds as the Jonker, the Lesotho, the Taylor-Burton, the Star of Sierra Leone, and the Star of Independence. He also presented the celebrated Hope, Portuguese, and Oppenheimer diamonds to the Smithsonian Institution as gifts to the American people. In jewelry, he created magic, bringing exceptional stones together in the finest of designs. Like the seventeenth-century French gem merchant and adventurer Jean-Baptiste Tavernier, Mr. Winston traveled all over the world in search of the biggest and best in diamonds and other fine gems.

For over fifty years, people have tried to understand the phenomenal success that Harry Winston experienced, to explain his perceptiveness in the cutting, buying, and selling of precious jewels. Yet his success resulted from what was actually a simple truth: he instinctively knew gemstones. Just as Michelangelo *knew* how to sculpt, Mozart *knew* how to compose music, and Benvenuto Cellini *knew* goldsmithing, Harry Winston *knew* gemstones. There was fundamentally no need for any of them to be taught; their abilities in their various endeavors were available to them from an early age. Of men with this capacity, Balzac wrote, "Laden with the results of their past, and in possession of the capacities they have developed in the course of their evolution . . . men are philosophers, or mathematicians, artists or savants from their very cradle." Harry Winston, in speaking of his instinct, said, ". . . ever since I was quite young, jewels have fascinated me. I think I must have been born with some knowledge of them."[1] The stories and photographs in this book illustrate time and again his undeniable sixth sense about gemstones.

To commemorate the fiftieth anniversary of the incorporation of the Harry Winston firm, this book is dedicated thoughtfully to the memory of this extraordinary man and the legacy he left.

NO STONE UNTURNED:

THE STORY OF HARRY WINSTON

"Talk to me, Harry Winston, tell me all about it!" [1]

MARILYN MONROE,
IN *GENTLEMEN PREFER BLONDES*

"People! Drama! Romance! Excitement! What more could you want?"[2] Harry Winston once summarized his extraordinary career with these words. His life was a series of adventures and intrigues revolving around a deep, instinctive love for precious gems and a fascination for the people who shaped the world of fine gemstones. Years of experience gave him a wealth of practical knowledge as well as penetrating insight into the intricacies of human nature. Even so, he never ceased to marvel how often odd twists of fate had helped him become the "king of diamonds."[3]

Harry Winston was born in New York City on March 1, 1896. Even at a very early age, he demonstrated an uncanny ability to judge fine stones: "When he was twelve, he spotted in a pawnshop window a tray of junk jewelry with the sign TAKE YOUR PICK—25¢. A ring set with a green stone set his heart pounding. He bought it, took it back to his father's shop, and announced to his astonished dad that he had purchased a two-carat emerald for a quarter. Two days later, Harry sold the same stone for $800."[4] This ability to estimate the weight and value of mounted stones with great accuracy was to serve him well in the decades to come, to the amazement—and chagrin—of many.

Harry Winston actually started in the jewelry trade at the age of fifteen in Los Angeles. His father had moved to California for health reasons and subsequently opened a jewelry store on Figueroa Street. The senior Winston was an easygoing man who was content with his small and cautious business. Harry Winston had different ideas. A resourceful purveyor and connoisseur of gems

Harry Winston stands at the window of his office on East 51st Street as a king's ransom in fine jewelry is prepared for the move of Harry Winston, Inc. to its current Fifth Avenue location. For security, Mr. Winston's insurance company insisted that the famous jeweler never allow a full view of his face to appear in publicity photographs.

Harry Winston (on the left) stands with his father and sister in his father's Los Angeles store in July 1911.

even in his early years, he would carry his father's wares from one saloon to the next, selling to newly affluent oil prospectors.

This resourcefulness became his hallmark when he returned to New York. In 1920, Harry Winston used the two thousand dollars he had saved while in California to set up what was at first a one-man firm, the Premier Diamond Company, in a small office at 535 Fifth Avenue.

Carving a niche for himself in New York's competitive gem industry was not easy. Young Harry Winston stretched his financial resources to the limit, tirelessly pursuing the rare buys in the wholesale marts and scouting for auction bargains. It was exhausting, time-consuming work, but after two years Winston had ten thousand dollars in savings and twenty thousand dollars' worth of jewels to show for his efforts. He was so confident in his growing business that he hired another person to help with the company. Unfortunately, Winston had not yet fully developed the keen knowledge of human nature that would help protect him in later years. One morning he arrived at the office to discover that his employee had disappeared with all of the company's assets. Harry Winston was ruined. Nevertheless, even though people in the trade had grown to know and respect his business acumen, and he received several generous job offers, Winston was determined to remain independent at any cost, to pursue his dream of becoming a major gem dealer.[5]

For the next few years, Harry Winston managed to make ends meet as a result of cautious deals and purchasing credits from a sympathetic bank. Recognizing the difficulties of breaking into the tightly controlled diamond market, he decided to look beyond the conventional sources of fine gems to what was then the unconventional: estate jewelry.

It is ironic that Harry Winston's career blossomed as the opulent fashions of the Victorian and Edwardian ages were in full decline, and it is a tribute to his ingenuity that he turned this decline so richly to his advantage. During the 1920s there was an abundance of estate jewelry on the market, costly pieces that people had begun to liquidate for a variety of reasons soon after World War I. The stomachers, corsage ornaments, ornate tiaras, diamond dog collars, and other jewels that had been the height of fashion during the late nineteenth and early twentieth centuries fell from favor. Such "antique" jewelry was usually sold at a fraction of its original price. Harry Winston's plan was to purchase the outdated pieces of jewelry and remove the gems, many of which were of the "old-mine" cut. He believed that by recutting the stones for greater sparkle and brilliancy, and then mounting them in more contemporary settings, he would appeal to the taste of the "modern" generation.

His first real break came in 1925, when he heard about a large collection of jewels that was being sold from the estate of Rebecca Darlington Stoddard, in New Haven, Connecticut. Mrs. Stoddard came from a wealthy Pittsburgh family. Her husband, Louis, from a wealthy New England family, was a famous polo player. Mr. Winston also learned that powerful dealer combines were bidding on the Stoddard collection, and got word of the approximate amount of the bids.

Acting on one of his characteristic hunches, he decided to make an offer for the collection himself. The president of a branch of the New Netherlands Bank (since absorbed by the Chase Manhattan Bank) had taken a liking to young Winston, and had helped carry him through the lean years with purchasing credits. Mr. Winston went to the president and asked him to write a letter of introduction to Mr. Stoddard, hoping that such credentials would secure him a personal interview. Armed with the highly complimentary letter, Winston arrived at the Stoddard estate, "Tenacres" (now Rosary Hall of Albertus Magnus College). The letter had its effect: Mr. Stoddard gave Harry Winston permission to appraise the collection.

Although penniless, Mr. Winston confidently offered Stoddard a million dollars for the collection—a figure higher than that of any of the combines. Mr. Stoddard was on the verge of accepting the bid when Winston, afraid of being turned down, hastily made a second proposal: "Give me six months," he said, "and I'll get you $200,000 more than the million. My commission will amount to $120,000, so you'll be ahead by $80,000." Mr. Stoddard readily agreed to the plan, and Winston set out to accomplish what seemed impossible. It took a great deal of salesmanship and perseverance, but within six months Winston had sold the collection to various jewel connoisseurs for a total of $1,250,000—$50,000 more than he had guaranteed Mr. Stoddard. His commission on the transaction was $125,000.[6]

With this money, quite an amount in 1925, the estate jewelry he sought was now within reach. By compiling a mailing list of names from the *Social Register* and *Who's Who*, supplemented by a list of leading judges and attorneys (who would be familiar with estates about to be probated), Harry Winston was able to offer his services to a wide range of people. In the course of his career, he was to handle the jewelry of many of the wealthiest individuals in the world.

In 1926, Harry Winston negotiated a purchase that would permanently establish him as a leader in the jewelry trade. The late Arabella Huntington (widow of Collis P. Huntington, the American railroad builder, and later the wife of his nephew, Henry Huntington) had owned a fabulous collection of jewels, famous for its beautiful diamonds and exquisite ropes of pearls. Soon after Winston arrived to bid on the collection he learned that her son, Archer M. Huntington, was a formidable negotiator. The appraisal took place in the Huntington vault. When Mr. Winston asked to take one of the diamond bracelets upstairs so that he could examine it under better lighting, Mr. Huntington replied that he would immediately raise the price of the bracelet from $120,000 to $130,000 if Winston removed it from the vault. Disregarding the costly proviso, Mr. Winston took the bracelet upstairs, where he determined that it was worth considerably more than even the higher price. Winston bid just over $1,200,000 for the entire collection.

Once again, he turned to his bank for financing. However, this time a meeting was set up with the board of directors, and did not include his friend from the local branch. He got off to a shaky start. With a jaunty cap on his head, he arrived late at the loan hearing. The bankers took the youthful-looking Harry Winston, who was small in stature and ruddy cheeked, for a messenger boy. "What do you want, boy?" they asked. He was ordered to return to his boss with instructions that the dealer was to appear in person if he wanted to conclude the transaction. Eventually, Winston's confidence and knowledge, along with his excellent record of past transactions with the bank, convinced the board of his integrity: The bank loaned him the money, requesting only its standard commission plus a small profit. Thus, Harry Winston got his loan and, consequently, the Huntington jewels. For many years thereafter, however, Mr. Winston was accompanied at such sessions by a tall, white-haired, distinguished-looking gentleman, who handled the formalities while Winston quietly guided the transactions.

Mr. Winston loved the Huntington jewels and delighted in talking about them. One of Mrs. Huntington's necklaces was a string of 160 pearls that was sixty inches long; it had cost Mrs. Huntington more than one million dollars to assemble. Ironically, she had gone blind by the time the necklace was finally completed. Mr. Winston split the necklace up after he acquired it and was fond of saying that at least two dozen women in various parts of the world now wore the Huntington pearls.

December of 1930 was a momentous month for Harry Winston. First, he successfully bid on a 39-carat emerald-cut diamond that was the largest diamond ever sold in a public auction in the United States up to that time. This stone had formerly been owned by Elenore Elverson, wife of Colonel James Elverson, Jr., former owner and publisher of the *Philadelphia Inquirer.*

Shortly thereafter, newspapers from coast to coast headlined the purchase of the jewelry from the "Lucky" Baldwin estate by Harry Winston. This collection had been assembled by Elias Jackson "Lucky" Baldwin and his daughter, Clara Baldwin Stocker. "Lucky" Baldwin drove a hansom cab in San Francisco before he successfully joined the California gold rush of 1849. He subsequently amassed a fortune in mining ventures, most notably the famous Comstock mines in Nevada. At his death in 1909, his ranch at Santa Anita, California, comprised over 25,000 acres. His collection of jewels included a 26-carat ruby that was rivaled in weight and quality by not more than half a dozen rubies in the world;* a

---

*This ruby was subsequently purchased by the American jewelry firm of Black, Starr, Frost-Gorham, who in turn sold it to industrialist J.P. Morgan in 1931. In 1937, his daughter sold it to Cartier, from whom it was purchased by Mrs.

25-carat marquise diamond; a 14-carat emerald-cut diamond; a 40-carat pear-shaped diamond (that served as a drop to a diamond necklace so long it had to be strung around the wearer's neck three times; otherwise, it would hang at the wearer's knees); and a tiara consisting of more than five hundred diamonds.

The manner in which Harry Winston purchased the Baldwin jewels was just as remarkable as the jewels themselves. As he told the story: "By the time I was thirteen or fourteen, my judgment of the quality of a gem was so sure, so instinctive, that my father counted on me to advise him."[7] Harry Winston's father was able to teach him about dollar values. But when it came to quality, the younger Winston was the teacher, not the student.

> "Soon jewelers became interested in my talent and were furthering my education. Each gem they showed me was like a friend, unique and unforgettable. When I was seventeen, a friend of my father's was sent a collection of jewels to clean, and he invited me to see them. I was thrilled. I looked at each piece carefully, noting the quality of the stones, the cutting, their beauty.
>
> "Fifteen years later, when I was a wholesaler in New York, my agent on the West Coast called me. He said he'd been offered a pretty nice collection of jewels and he thought I should come out and take a look at it. He began describing the pieces and I interrupted him after he'd listed three. 'Buy it,' I said. He stuttered something about how I really must see it first, that it was a big collection, a big purchase. 'Buy it,' I said. 'I know every piece in it.' I did, too. I began describing them to him. I could see each stone in my mind's eye. It was the same collection I had studied with such pleasure when I was a young man."[8]

With his successes in estate jewelry, Harry Winston achieved financial independence. Now, the banks came to him. By 1932, in

---

Horace Dodge (then Mrs. Stillman). The stone appeared at auction in Geneva in May of 1971, and has since been recut from its original weight of 26.12 carats. It has been called the Thibaw ruby (after King Thibaw of Burma, 1878–1885) as the result of a statement made by Mr. Winston in 1930 to the effect that although little is known of its early history, it probably came from a Burmese king.

This diamond bracelet is one of the many fine pieces from the estate of Mrs. Emma T. Gary.

addition to buying and selling estate pieces, he had started manufacturing his own jewelry. In that year, he closed the Premier Diamond Company and incorporated under the name Harry Winston.

In his 1936 purchase of the estate of Mrs. Emma T. Gary (the widow of Judge Elbert T. Gary, who was chairman of the board at U.S. Steel for many years in the early twentieth century), Winston demonstrated the practical value of his ability to appraise mounted stones quickly and accurately. The estate was so vast that most of the experts who were invited to bid on it spent three or four days examining the incredible collection of matched round diamonds in earrings, bracelets, necklaces, and rings. One necklace, over six feet long, contained 166 round diamonds, each weighing approximately one carat. Mr. Winston raced through the collection—a total of seventy-nine pieces—in *three hours,* coming up with a bid that topped his most optimistic competitor.

Harry Winston's almost unerring instincts about gemstones grew over the years to legendary proportions. He had an uncanny ability to look at a stone and know exactly what could be created from it. What others saw as risks, Winston considered opportunities. In 1975, almost seventy years after his first emerald "find," his intuition and optimism came through for him with the Star of Sierra Leone. Mr. Winston had originally had the 143-carat* emer-

---

*For simplicity, weights in this and the other introductory sections have been rounded off to the nearest whole carat. Precise carat weights of those stones featured in the "Empire Built on Diamonds" section are included in the individual entries.

ald-cut diamond fashioned from a rough stone, an exciting prospect, as it was to have been the largest diamond of his career. (The Jonker diamond had been 149 carats originally, but was recut to 125 carats to give it a more oblong outline.) Although Mr. Winston knew that the Star of Sierra Leone would not be perfect when he originally had it cut, he eventually decided that only a flawless stone of such size would be good enough for him. He ordered the top of the stone, which contained the imperfections, to be sawed off. Many thought him crazy to attempt such a maneuver. As always, though, he was confident of his decision. The bottom section that remained was refashioned to a 33-carat D-flawless emerald cut. From the top piece, he was able to fashion six diamonds, of which five were D-flawless, with a total weight of 21 carats. These six stones were used to create a flower pin with diamond "petals." The seven diamonds cut from the Star of Sierra Leone carried a significantly larger value than the original flawed stone.

The Star of Sierra Leone pin.

While his achievements brought him hosts of admirers, Harry Winston's greatest admirer was his wife Edna, whom he married in 1933. Their unconventional courtship proved to be only the preamble to the rest of their adventurous life together. The couple had been courting for some time, and Edna was deeply attached to Harry. But she felt somewhat distressed by his preoccupation with his rapidly growing diamond business. So the relationship was broken off, and eventually Edna became engaged to another man.

Two days before her wedding, Edna got a call from Harry, who was in Florida selling jewels. Although they had not seen each other for a year, after talking for only a few minutes Harry insisted that she marry him instead. Still leery of his consuming passion for diamonds, Edna warily consented to his proposal on the condition that the wedding take place immediately. Harry Winston arrived in New York the next day and they were married. He then brought his bride back to Palm Beach, and immediately resumed selling jewels. In fact, he spent most of their honeymoon telling Edna about his dream of the big diamonds he would someday buy. His enthusiasm proved contagious, and Edna soon found herself sharing a life full of diamonds and adventure.

Certainly one of their most exciting and dangerous experiences together occurred at the outbreak of World War II, when Mr. and Mrs. Winston found themselves in the south of France. The two million dollars' worth of diamonds Mr. Winston had in jewelry stores in the Riviera were no longer insured, as Lloyd's of London had canceled all such policies when the fighting started. Harry Winston had to get the jewels out quickly and with only his wife's help. Within a few hours of learning that Germany had declared war, he had all the jewels in hand.

"For the life of me I couldn't think of any clever way to hide those stones so that no one would be the wiser," Mr. Winston said. "What I finally did was so crazy that I laugh when I think of it."[9]

He put what he could in the heels of his shoes and those of his wife. Some of the jewels he knotted into strips of cloth and pinned inside his trouser legs. The remainder were very cleverly—if uncomfortably—hidden in several wiglets within his wife's hair. Their trip from the Riviera to the seaport of Le Havre was a nightmare. They slept in their clothes and shoes for two weeks. Even after arriving in Le Havre, they had to wait out several air-raids before they finally sailed. Once at sea, Mrs. Winston eagerly looked forward to changing her clothes and washing her hair, as soon as all the items were put in the ship's vault. At first, Mr. Winston insisted that the diamonds stay where they were. "But Edna was adamant. Two million dollars or not, she said, she wasn't going to look like a fright any longer with all those wiglets in her hair. I thought it was very unfair of her, for she's a beautiful woman with or without the wiglets," Mr. Winston commented much later. "However, I gave in and put the jewels in the ship's safe. But if we'd been torpedoed, I would have never forgiven myself for yielding to a woman's vanity."[10]

> "My father was always afraid that jewels would someday possess me. He was satisfied with just a small neighborhood jewelry business uptown, but I was always interested in larger stones. He used to say to me, 'Harry, you're the master of your jewels now, but if you keep on buying such big stones, someday your jewels will master you.' Sometimes, I think he was right."[11]

At times, Harry Winston had a deeply emotional feeling toward great gems. When he held a rough diamond in his hand, he could see the fire and beauty that lay under its frosty coating. He would check and recheck all fine diamonds as they were being polished. When one was finished, he would often call for it from the safe, examining it for hours. When, in 1954, he cut the 62-carat flawless pear-shaped diamond that eventually was named the Winston, he insisted, "I'm going to keep this one quiet. I want to keep it to myself. This stone is like a great painting. You want to keep on looking at it."[12] Sometimes, he would keep a large diamond in the pocket of his suit jacket, rolling it between his fingers as he spoke to clients. Before its sale for four million dollars in 1977, Mr. Winston occasionally kept the 76-carat Star of Independence in his pocket. In its time, it was probably the most expensive touchstone in the world. When one of his large gems was eventually sold, Mr. Winston would experience a great sense of loss—that is, until he "adopted" another. *Life* magazine once described Harry Winston as a "reverent connoisseur with so deep a love for fine stones that the sale of a top quality diamond often suffuses him with a gentle melancholy for days."[13]

On one occasion when Mrs. Winston was trying on a beautiful pair of earrings in front of her husband, he remarked with a gleam in his eye that he hated to see a woman get any of his diamonds. Mrs. Winston laughed knowingly. "Oh Harry! Always complaining about selling your babies!"[14]

Harry Winston himself often had occasion to wonder whether he was a merchant or a collector. One day the Maharaja of Baroda came to him to purchase some jewelry. Within a short while, Mr. Winston had sold the maharaja several million dollars' worth of jewels. But his reaction to the huge sale was not typical of such a successful businessman. "When Harry came home that evening I thought he was ill," said Edna Winston. "He seemed so unhappy and depressed. It turned out that he had taken leave of some of his favorite pieces of jewelry."[15]

In the same vein, if Harry Winston was determined to have a stone, he would not let it slip from his grasp. The Winstons were in Paris one summer when a particularly beautiful diamond caught Mr. Winston's fancy. He decided to buy the stone immediately, but the weather was so warm in the city that Edna persuaded him to take her to Deauville for the weekend first. They returned to discover that "his" diamond had been sold to someone else. Six months later, Mr. Winston found the same stone in New York. Without hesitation, he purchased it for sixty thousand dollars more than it had been offered to him in Paris.

This 104.40-carat pear-shaped emerald is the largest faceted gem emerald on public record.

Yet Harry Winston's fascination and love for beautiful gems was not limited to diamonds. Some of his most interesting transactions involved rubies, sapphires and, in particular, emeralds. Eva Stotesbury was a name that dominated the American social scene for the first forty years of this century. Her fabulous 34.40-carat hexagon-shaped emerald, as well as the legendary emerald tiara that held it, were sold to Mr. Winston in 1943. (The first known appearance of this stone was in 1908, when Evalyn Walsh McLean saw it hanging on a necklace with the 95-carat pear-shaped diamond known as the Star of the East.[16]) The hexagon-shaped emerald known as the "Stotesbury" was mounted as a ring and sold in 1947 to Mrs. May Bonfils Stanton, daughter of the publisher and co-founder of the *Denver Post*. Although most of her large collection of jewelry was auctioned in New York in 1962, this ring was not included and its present whereabouts are not known.

In 1948, a 61.94-carat emerald called the Catherine the Great was purchased from the estate of Canadian socialite Melba McMartin Van Buren,* who had inherited it from her father, industrialist Duncan McMartin. Originally, this emerald had belonged to one of the most astute jewelry collectors in pre–World War I Europe, the Grand Duchess Vladimir, sister-in-law to the last tsar of Russia, Nicholas II. (The diamond tiara with interchangeable cabochon emeralds or pearl drops worn so often by Queen Elizabeth II of England had also belonged to the Grand Duchess Vladimir.) After her death in Switzerland in 1920, her children sold many of her jewelry pieces, including the large emerald. Mr. Winston mounted the emerald as a ring, and gave it on memo to King Farouk of Egypt in 1951. Two days after the emerald arrived in Alexandria, a revolution forced the king to abdicate. Just

---

*Among the important items Mr. Winston purchased was a cushion-shaped stone of 54.75 carats—the Van Buren diamond. The Van Buren was sold that same year to an Indian client. It resurfaced in New York in December of 1970, when it was auctioned as part of the estate of Vala Byfield.

This 68.12-carat emerald has belonged to Abdul Hamid II of Turkey, Princess Anastasia of Greece, and the Maharaja of Nawanagar. In 1966, it was sold to a European gem connoisseur.

before he fled the country, he gave the United States ambassador the as-yet-unpaid-for emerald, instructing him to have it delivered to Harry Winston in New York. The ring was subsequently sold in 1953 to a client from Texas.

In 1959, Mr. Winston purchased 17 emeralds weighing a total of 256.30 carats from the Maharaja of Nawanagar (a small but wealthy princely state in the south of India). The collection included several stones with an interesting pedigree and became what Mr. Winston felt was one of the greatest disappointments of his career. The largest stone in the collection, a superb one, weighed 68.12 carats. It had once belonged to the last sultan of the Ottoman Empire, Abdul Hamid II, whose collection of gemstones was rivaled by few. After Hamid's abdication in 1909, an auction of his collection was held in Paris, a sale that literally flooded Europe with superb gemstones of all description. Cartier purchased a number of the stones including the aforementioned. They sold a collection of emeralds to Princess Anastasia of Greece (formerly Mrs. Nancy Leeds, widow of American tin magnate William Leeds). After her death in 1926, the stones were repurchased by Cartier. Six of the largest, weighing a total of 224.08 carats, were used to form part of an emerald and diamond necklace that was sold to the Maharaja of Nawanagar; these emeralds were among the 17 that Mr. Winston purchased from the maharaja in 1959, the two largest stones weighing 69.15 carats (later recut to 68.12 carats) and 50.50 carats (later recut to 49.68 carats). With the collection, one necklace was designed from which a necklace as well as three clips and a pair of earrings could be created. The price in 1960 was one and a half million dollars. Although several clients expressed interest in the piece, only one South American seriously negotiated for it. After much discussion, the man felt that he would rather place the money in something that was a "sure" investment. (By 1972, the value of the largest stone alone was greater than the original asking price of the entire necklace.) Eventually, the 68.12-carat stone was sold to a European connoisseur, mounted in the necklace pictured on page 18, and the 49.68-carat gem was sold as a pendant to a diamond necklace. Mr. Winston often spoke regretfully of the original client who turned down this fabulous offer.

In 1965, a 142.00-carat squarish emerald of unknown pedigree was purchased by Harry Winston. The stone was lovely, but Mr. Winston felt that it would be enhanced appreciably if it were recut to remove the imperfections, which were concentrated along the outer edges. Recut it was, to a pear shape of 104.40 carats; the stone became a piece for legends, and is the largest recorded faceted gem emerald known. Pictured on page 17, it was sold to an American industrialist, repurchased by Harry Winston in 1974, and is now in the private collection of a king.

This photograph was taken in 1949 to publicize the Court of Jewels. On her forehead the model is wearing the Hope diamond; around her neck, the Earl of Dudley necklace and the Inquisition necklace; the Indore pear shapes lie on either side of the Star of the East. At her waist is the Jonker diamond; the 337-carat Catherine the Great sapphire graces her wrist while the Mabel Boll and McLean diamonds are shown on her left hand.

"I want the public to know more about precious gems," Winston explained. "With so much expensive junk jewelry around these days, people forget that a good diamond, ruby, or emerald, however small, is a possession to be prized for generations."[17]

Exhibitions of Harry Winston jewelry have raised millions of dollars for various charities since 1949. That year, Mr. Winston found himself with a number of important large diamonds and historical pieces of jewelry. Some of the diamonds he himself had cut, while other diamonds and historical pieces had been purchased in the aftermath of World War II, when many individuals converted prized heirlooms into much-needed funds. This superb collection enabled Harry Winston to combine a lifelong wish to educate people about gemstones with a desire to sponsor charitable exhibitions. He had always wanted the public to know more about precious gems, so that they could share his appreciation for them. He wanted them to understand that, unlike costume or inferior jewelry, fine gemstones were ageless, enduring treasures that could be prized for generations. To this end, Mr. Winston created an unprecedented exhibit called the Court of Jewels. The exhibit was first displayed at a benefit for the United Hospital Fund in Rockefeller Center, New York City, from November 23 to December 30, 1949. Outside of the British Crown Jewels on display in the Tower of London, the general public had seldom been given the opportunity to view such a fabulous collection.

For four years, from 1949 to 1953, the Court of Jewels toured the major cities of America. In the spring of 1951, for example, the Court went on tour for the benefit of the National Foundation for Infantile Paralysis (now the March of Dimes Birth Defects Foundation). The glittering array included the 46-carat Hope diamond, the

The Inquisition necklace.

95-carat Star of the East, the 94-carat pair of diamonds known as the Indore pear shapes, the 126-carat Jonker emerald-cut diamond, the 31-carat McLean diamond, the 46-carat Mabel Boll diamond, and the 337-carat Catherine the Great sapphire. Also included in the exhibition was the emerald and diamond Inquisition necklace, with a history that started with the Spanish plunder of the Incas, when the emeralds—including the 44-carat barrel-shaped gem used as the center stone—first came to light. The necklace was originally owned by Spanish royalty, then by members of the French court. At the turn of the century, it was purchased by an Indian maharaja. Harry Winston obtained the necklace in 1947; it was later sold and then donated by the purchaser to the Smithsonian Institution, Washington, D.C., where it is now on permanent display. Also included was the Earl of Dudley necklace, with rich green emeralds linked, festooned, and looped together with diamonds. This necklace was originally worn by ladies of the Spanish court, had come into the possession of the Earl of Dudley at the beginning of this century, and had then passed to an Indian maharaja before it was purchased by Harry Winston in 1947.

At different times in the four-year history of the Court of Jewels, several of the pieces were sold. Mr. Winston always obtained exquisite items to take their place. By the mid-1950s, however, the various costs involved in such an exhibit became prohibitive, and the Court of Jewels was disbanded. Subsequent public exhibits featured only one or a few of the superb Harry Winston pieces that had once comprised the spectacular "Court." The Hope diamond continued to be used for various charity affairs and exhibitions until 1958, when Mr. Winston donated it to the Smithsonian Institution as a gift to the American people.

Harry Winston's prodigious memory and affinity for gems generated a keen interest in how many times he had owned the same stone—be it diamond, ruby, emerald, or sapphire.

COURTESY OF THE SMITHSONIAN INSTITUTION—DANE PENLAND, PHOTOGRAPHER.

The 90-carat Briolette, as worn by Mrs. I. W. Killam.

Although the journey of a stone from one owner to another always fascinated him, he seemed to feel a sense of pride when it returned "home" once again.

Several interesting examples of this occurred in conjunction with Mr. Winston's purchase of the jewelry of one astute collector, Dorothy Killam. The widow of wealthy Canadian financier Isaac W. Killam, Mrs. Killam had accumulated over some years jewelry that ultimately represented one of the finest private collections in the world. Dorothy Killam made headlines in America in the late 1950s when she, an ardent Brooklyn Dodgers baseball fan, tried to buy the team to keep it from moving to Los Angeles. After Mrs. Killam died in July 1965, the bulk of her one-hundred-million-dollar estate was bequeathed to the Canada Council, the Montreal Neurological Institute, and universities throughout Canada.

The major jewelry pieces of Mrs. Killam's estate were all created by Harry Winston. Among the highlights were two oriental pearl necklaces that must rank among the finest in the world. One was a two-strand necklace of seventy pearls with an 11-carat oval pink diamond as the clasp. The other was a three-strand necklace of 209 pearls with a 10-carat round pink diamond clasp. She also owned the 39-carat sky blue Crown of Charlemagne diamond and the 90-carat Briolette, as well as earrings with two pear-shaped diamond drops weighing a total of 33 carats. Her exquisite pair of diamond bracelets, a birthday present from her husband, contained a total of 278 carats in stones.

Mrs. Killam also owned what are, at about 20 carats each, perhaps the largest diamond stud earrings in the world. Interestingly, Mr. Winston had obtained one of the stones, set in a ruby and diamond pendant, from the estate of Evalyn Walsh McLean, owner of the Hope diamond. In 1949, he had the diamond removed and set in a ring, which was sold in 1950 to an American client. Upon the death of the client in 1957, the stone once again came into Mr. Winston's possession. As fate would have it, this

The five pear-shaped diamonds in this necklace designed for Mrs. I. W. Killam weigh a total of 83 carats.

stone matched beautifully with a diamond he had recently finished cutting, and Mrs. Killam had just mentioned her desire to buy something special. (This occurred often throughout Mr. Winston's career: the right stones turning up again in the right place at the right time.)

Another important piece in Mrs. Killam's collection was a necklace of round and baguette diamonds weighing a total of 62 carats, with five pear-shaped diamonds (weighing a total of 83 carats) suspended from it. One of these pear shapes had come from a twin pear shape ring that, again, had once belonged to Evalyn Walsh McLean. The other four pear shapes (the largest was over 20 carats and the smallest almost 14 carats) had been traded in by the Duke and Duchess of Windsor late in 1950. Mrs. Killam's lovely necklace was assembled in January of 1951. After its purchase from the estate in 1967, the necklace portion was sold separately. The five pear-shaped diamonds were recut for greater clarity and brilliance. After repolishing, each stone received a D- or E-flawless certificate. The two smallest stones were sold in 1972 as drops to diamond earrings. The three remaining diamonds were sold as rings; of course, with the hope that Mr. Winston would see them again.

Harry Winston's sharp business sense and incurable optimism were important keys to his success. Knowledgeable and perceptive, as well as personable, he was a natural salesman. But the heart of his business, and of the man himself, was his deep appreciation of each stone as a unique object of beauty and art.

Once Harry Winston observed one of his salesmen as he showed a beautiful diamond to a wealthy Dutch merchant. Although the customer listened with some interest to the salesman's description, he ultimately turned away, saying, "It's a wonderful stone, but not exactly what I want."

Winston intercepted the customer as he was departing and asked, "Do you mind if I show you that diamond once more?"

The merchant agreed, and Winston, without repeating a word the salesman had said, took the stone in his hand and simply extolled its virtues as an object of deep and lasting beauty. The customer abruptly changed his mind and purchased the stone. Later, while he was waiting for the diamond to be brought to him, he turned to Winston and said "Why did I buy it willingly from you, though I had no difficulty in saying no to your salesman?" Winston replied, "This salesman is one of the best men in the business. He *knows* diamonds—but I *love* them."[18]

As Harry Winston's vision of gems knew no creative bounds, so did his optimism know no limits. "If a man thinks big, he will be big—in thinking small, he settles for mediocrity" was his oft-spoken philosophy. It served him particularly well on one occasion when he happened to be in Geneva at the same time as King Saud. The Winston office received a message that His Highness would like Mr. Winston to show him some jewels. The king purchased a number of important items, the entire transaction amounting to several million dollars.

As Mr. Winston was leaving, one of the king's aides approached to inquire if he had any diamond bracelets, as the king was interested in buying six. But, because the king was departing the next morning at 8:30, someone would have to deliver the jewelry to him by 6 a.m. Mr. Winston sent a messenger ahead with the king's request. Upon his return to the office, he found that the staff had assembled the six most important bracelets. "Just six!" he exclaimed. "Bring me all the diamond bracelets we have." The staff then debated as to who was going to call on the king at 6 a.m. Mr. Winston said that, of course, *he* would. The next morning, he arrived promptly at 6 a.m. with fifty-five diamond bracelets. While the king ate breakfast and reviewed the sparkling array, Mr. Winston waited patiently. An aide then came down and told him the king would buy *all* fifty-five. One can imagine the reaction when Mr. Winston returned to the office, literally empty-handed, and then the surprise the next morning when a message came saying that the king needed twenty-five more! From an inquiry for six diamond bracelets, Mr. Winston sold eighty, all because he followed his own advice and thought big.

Harry Winston felt that much of his success lay in his judgment of people. At times, he would give two or three pieces of jewelry worth several hundred thousand dollars to a new customer without as much as a signature. Often, the customer would appear at the store at nine the next morning, not having slept the whole night. One customer told Mr. Winston that he was up all night worrying that Mr. Winston was worrying.

Some years ago, Mr. Winston showed one of his clients a beautiful ring in his London office. The two of them then went out for tea at a fashionable restaurant, taking the ring along with them. The woman tried the ring on several times as they chatted. Finally she rose to leave, the ring still on her finger. By dinner time the client was calling frantically all over the West End of London, trying to locate Harry Winston. She finally reached him while he was dining at a restaurant. He assured her that he knew she had left with the ring, but had not felt the need to say anything. "You're just a damn fool," cried the exasperated lady. "No," he replied calmly, "I know how to evaluate people."[19]

Mr. Winston particularly enjoyed relating the following incident concerning a 20-carat D-flawless marquise. At first, the stone was not looked on with any special regard, as Harry Winston was responsible for cutting more than two hundred diamonds in the 20-carat range. Late one Friday afternoon in 1965, several months after the stone was mounted as a ring, the diamond assumed an entirely new character. A customer well known to Mr. Winston arrived at the salon, accompanied by a beautiful, statuesque

In his palm, Harry Winston holds (from left to right, top to bottom): the 95-carat Star of the East diamond, the 45-carat Hope diamond, the 70-carat Idol's Eye diamond, one of the Indore pear shapes, a 62-carat emerald once owned by the Grand Duchess Vladimir of Russia, the 126-carat Jonker diamond, the 337-carat Catherine the Great sapphire, a 14-carat Burma ruby, and the other Indore pear shape (the two Indore diamonds weigh a total of 94 carats).

blonde who clearly was not his wife. With much fanfare, he selected the above-mentioned stone. Knowing that the man could well afford to pay, Mr. Winston gave him the ring on memo. Mr. Winston always delighted in recounting how, the following Monday morning, the customer returned the diamond saying, "Thanks, I had the most wonderful weekend of my life. I'll make it up to you soon." Until the stone was later sold to a well-married American client, it was reverently referred to as the Weekend diamond.

At all costs, Mr. Winston considered the anonymity and privacy of the client sacred. The extent to which he held to this credo is illustrated by a visit in 1947 of the Duke and Duchess of Windsor. Winston's desk was literally covered with the many fine jewels he showed them: diamonds, rubies, emeralds, sapphires, and pearls. It is common knowledge that the Duchess of Windsor was an ardent admirer of great jewelry, and had a fabulous personal collection. Few people, however, realize that the duke shared this passion. Mr. Winston spent several hours discussing not only what he was showing them, but also the great jewels of the British royal family. After they left, Mr. Winston went home to dinner. At about nine that night, he got a call from some people at the office. They were in a panic, as the nightly inventory had disclosed that a 55-carat diamond was missing, one of the very items Winston had been showing the royal couple that afternoon.

Harry Winston grabbed a taxi back down Fifth Avenue and called the Holmes Company to arrange for the opening of the safe in his office. As Mr. Winston later related:

> "We could not find a trace of it! What we went through! The next day, the insurance people wanted to ask the duke and duchess if they remembered seeing the diamond, but I said no; they

BERNARD HOFFMAN, *LIFE*, © 1952 TIME, INC.

could talk to anybody else but *not* to the duke and duchess. I told them I'd take the financial responsibility. The insurance company wouldn't have to absorb the loss. Anything, as long as they didn't bother the Windsors. I wouldn't allow anything that might cast suspicion on them. We kept searching the entire building. We went through all our wastepapers. Fifty-five carats! It couldn't be missing! It was big enough to trip over! We all went through agony for weeks. It was a reflection on everyone in the firm. My secretary, of course, was a nervous wreck.

"Three months later, a customer came in and bought a pearl necklace, so I asked my secretary to bring an empty jewel case. She brought the case in, and when I opened it, there was the diamond! It had fallen in while I was showing all those things to the duke and duchess. So you see, I was right. It would have been a dreadful thing if we had let the insurance investigators go around and bother the Duke and Duchess of Windsor."[20]

In the course of his long career, Mr. Winston claimed to have had major problems with only one customer, King Farouk of Egypt. For some years, Mr. Winston had considerable dealings with King Farouk. In late 1951, shortly after Farouk had purchased the 125-carat Jonker diamond from Mr. Winston, he bought the 95-carat Star of the East and a deep green round diamond of 70 carats called the Lal Qila. Although he had paid cash for the Jonker, he placed the other two stones on account. Not many months later, the king also took on memo the 62-carat emerald that had once belonged to the Russian Crown Jewels and was known as the Catherine the Great. Two days after the emerald arrived in Alexandria, a revolution forced King Farouk to abdicate. Just before he fled the country, he gave U.S. Ambassador Cafferey the as-yet-unpaid-for emerald, instructing him to deliver it to Harry Winston in New York. In the summer of 1952, Mr. Winston met the king in Capri and was told that not only had he left the diamonds behind, but he also did not have the money to pay for them. Since Farouk had returned the emerald, and legal action against the now-deposed king appeared to be pointless, Mr. Winston let the matter drop. A short time later, however, Harry Winston learned that the former king had both the Star of the East and the money to pay for it as well. It then took Mr. Winston more than ten years of litigation to obtain access to a safe deposit box in Switzerland and retrieve the 95-carat D-color diamond. Despite all of his efforts, the Lal Qila was never found or returned; in 1961, it was "written off" the company records. To this day, no trace of it has been uncovered.

Because Harry Winston had to deal with many different types of people throughout the world, he developed a sensitivity to their various customs and cultural practices. Westerners are generally unaware of the extent to which astrology rules the lives of many people in the Near East and India. Mr. Winston learned this lesson early in his career. In 1937, while vacationing in Florida, Mr. Winston and his wife received a telegram from an Indian prince who was on holiday in France. A large ruby in which Mr. Winston had expressed interest was for sale, but only if it was purchased by noon on a date less than a week away. The Winstons immediately flew to New York, where they hastily made connections with the Queen Mary, which was sailing for Europe that day. With all of their efforts, they arrived at the prince's chateau near Paris just past the designated noon deadline. Mr. Winston was congratulating himself on completing the trip so quickly, when the prince's aide told him that he was too late, that the stone was no longer available. If they would wait in Paris, though, they would be contacted when the situation changed. Three weeks later, a very impatient Harry Winston received a call that the stone was again for sale. It was then that he was told that the stars had foretold much unhappiness if the prince kept the ruby, but that he could sell it only during certain periods. The Winstons had missed the first period by half an hour!

Just after World War II, despite nine months of negotiation with another Indian prince over some pink and blue diamonds that

This diamond necklace is part of the three "sweet 16" sets designed by Harry Winston, Inc. in 1977 as a gift to a young princess from her father. The center stone is a 44-carat marquise. The bracelet and earrings shown on page 15 were also part of this gift.

the prince wished to buy, the stars again determined policy. In the few hours it took in the 1940s to reconnect a call to India, the prince entered into an unlucky time to buy gems. Mr. Winston had to wait another four months before all the celestial signs were correct to conclude the sale.

In 1977, the stars caused a major stir. In the fall of that year, an order was received to create three fabulous sets of jewelry—two of diamonds and one of emeralds—as a "sweet 16" gift to a princess from her father. When the three sets were completed, one of the diamond necklaces had a 44-carat marquise in its center, the other a 29-carat pear shape. The center of the third necklace was a superb 36-carat oval emerald. The accompanying earrings, bracelets, and rings were equally opulent. Not quite a month later, the number one wife, jealous of this lavish gift, asked the husband to have something created for her. He agreed and placed an order with Harry Winston for a third diamond set, on one condition: The jewels had to be designed, fabricated, and delivered in exactly six weeks. After that time, the stars would not be right, and there would be no deal; it was six weeks or nothing. Mr. Winston immediately put his staff to work around the clock to finish the entire set, understanding fully the significance of the conditions. The result was a necklace that had as its center the 51-carat Étoile du Désert and represented a total diamond weight of over 253 carats, a bracelet, earrings, and a 40-carat E-flawless emerald-cut diamond ring. The entire order was delivered with hardly a minute to spare. The necklace alone sold for over five million dollars.

With the death of Harry Winston in December of 1978, the world lost one of the most important and colorful diamond connoisseurs of modern times. He had a combination of skills and abilities that was as rare as many of the pieces of jewelry he created.

AN EMPIRE BUILT ON DIAMONDS

"No two diamonds are alike. Each diamond has a different nature. Each diamond has different problems. Each diamond must be handled as you handle a person."[1]

HARRY WINSTON

At one time or another, Harry Winston owned more than one-third of all the famous diamonds known to the world today. This section presents, in some cases for the first time, detailed descriptions and histories of some of these magnificent stones as well as two unique pieces of historically significant jewelry. Some of these named stones are relatively new to the world of fine jewels; their histories are just beginning. Others are surrounded by decades and even centuries of legend, their mystique growing with the passing years, as the stones themselves seem to affect the lives and destinies of the people who cherish them. Separating fact from fiction has, at times, been quite difficult, complicated by the absence of accurate records and the tendency of the media to exaggerate the already fanciful stories. Nevertheless, legend is an integral part of the mystique of many of the gems presented in the entries that follow, and has been included along with the verifiable histories of these stones to present as complete an account as possible.

There seems to be no hard-and-fast rule as to how a diamond acquires a name. In some cases, it assumes the moniker of one of its owners, as with the Hope or the Taylor-Burton. In others, the stone is named in honor of an event, as with the Deal Sweetener and the Star of Independence. In 1976, for example, the United States launched a satellite on a mission to photograph Mars. At that time, Harry Winston owned a 12.03-carat round pink diamond. The color of the stone was so intense that Ronald Winston christened it the Martian Pink in honor of the red planet. The 75-carat emerald cut known as the Buttercup (sold as a pendant in 1958) and the 72-carat emerald cut called the Dandelion (sold as a

These two green diamonds, weighing a total of 35 carats, are among the largest green diamonds ever recorded. They were sold to an Indian maharaja.

pendant in 1957) were aptly named because of their intense canary-yellow color. The name of a stone may also change when ownership is transferred, as was the case with the Ice Queen diamond. Stavros Niarchos purchased the 128-carat D-flawless Ice Queen in 1956; since then the stone has been referred to as the Niarchos.

Mr. Winston also handled many stones that, despite their unusual size, shape, or color, were never given a name. In 1938, he fashioned a 60-carat yellow emerald-cut diamond that was sold in 1940—unnamed. In 1948, Winston purchased two magnificent diamond bracelets from an Indian maharaja. The center stone of each bracelet was a round green diamond, with a total of 35 carats for both stones. The two green diamonds were reset as a pair of earrings and sold to another Indian maharaja in 1950. Neither stone was ever named.

At the same time that he purchased the bracelets, Winston also bought a superb emerald-and-diamond necklace that had an intense yellow 55-carat diamond as its center stone. Recut to 43 carats to bring out its full brilliance, the diamond was sold as a ring in 1952. In 1954, Mr. Winston purchased a 35-carat hexagon-shaped diamond. Three years later he purchased two other stones, each about 37 carats, cut in the same unusual shape. All three of these stones were sold to a single client to be used as pendants to necklaces. As with the yellow stone, this is believed to be the first time these large hexagon-shaped diamonds have been reported in the literature. They, too, remain nameless.

Also in 1954, Mr. Winston purchased a maharaja's treasure of previously unknown diamonds from an Indian dealer. This purchase included a 51-carat flawless emerald cut sold as a ring in 1959; two 21-carat pear shapes, which sold as drops to earrings in 1954; and a 44-carat pear shape sold as a ring in 1955. Mr. Winston sold a 19-carat intense pink flawless emerald-cut diamond in 1975. The following year, he sold the same client a 20-carat intense blue emerald-cut diamond. The client wears the two diamonds as earrings. Again, none of these extraordinary stones carries a title for the public record.

These unique blue and white diamond earrings, created in 1985, contain two interchangeable drops: a 7.08-carat blue emerald-cut diamond and a 7.38-carat F-color emerald-cut diamond.

In addition to selling exquisite faceted gems, Mr. Winston was very much involved in buying and cutting rough stones. His most spectacular diamond purchase occurred in 1974, when he bought a parcel of rough diamonds from Harry Oppenheimer (the chairman of De Beers Consolidated Mines, Ltd.) for $24,500,000—the largest individual sale of diamonds in history. Winston had these rough diamonds fashioned into stones that would become material for legends.

Unlike most of his compatriots in the diamond industry, Harry Winston sought to obtain the largest stones—not just the greatest number—possible from a single piece of rough. With the discovery of the South African diamond fields in the 1860s and the concomitant rise of a new industrial wealthy class, both the material and the broader market for large gems became available. Harry Winston was the first to systematically produce large, and in many cases, flawless diamonds. His efforts resulted in an inventory of stones that was, outside of a few royal collections, unrivaled in the world.

Many of Harry Winston's anecdotes make it seem as though large, flawless diamonds are plentiful, perhaps even commonplace. In reality, a combination of unusual factors and circumstances must be taken into account in order to fully appreciate the rarity of these gemstones. To get some idea of how rare diamonds truly are, it is useful to look at some mining figures. Of the total number of rough diamonds mined each year, less than twenty percent can be used in jewelry; the other eighty percent are sold for industrial use. For every unit of diamond recovered, over three million units of kimberlite (the rock in which diamond occurs) must be mined: one ounce of diamond to every hundred tons of rock. In alluvial deposits, the ratio is one ounce of diamond to fourteen hundred tons of gravel. To obtain one ounce of diamond that might be suitable for faceting, five thousand tons of rock must be excavated. After this precious ounce of gem-quality rough is retrieved, approximately two-thirds of it will become dust when the stone is shaped and polished.

In addition to size (carat weight), clarity and color are also important factors in determining a diamond's value. (These three factors—together with the cut of the stone—constitute the "four C's" on which the value of a diamond is determined.) In 1953, the Gemological Institute of America formulated a system for color grading cut diamonds. This system uses letters to represent color in a diamond, beginning with D for colorless and proceeding down through the alphabet. Clarity is assigned on the basis of the appearance of the stone when viewed with ten power magnification. Clarity grades range from flawless, to very, very slightly imperfect (VVS_1 and VVS_2), down to heavily flawed stones in which the imperfections can be viewed by the naked eye. Thus, a diamond might be certified D-flawless, or E-VVS_1, or F-flawless, depending on the combination of color and clarity it represents.

A diamond graded D-flawless is extremely rare. Of the twenty percent of rough diamonds that are suitable for use in jewelry, fewer than one percent have the *potential* to receive the D (colorless) rating. Of that one percent, only a fraction have the potential to become flawless stones; to obtain one ounce of diamonds with this potential, at least *five hundred thousand tons* of kimberlite must be mined.

The cutters and polishers have the final responsibility for creating a brilliant stone by shaping and redefining the rough to take maximum advantage of its potential. The natural crystal shape for diamond is an eight-sided double pyramid (octahedron). The object in cutting the rough material is to divide a diamond's natural shape and surface to obtain the maximum brilliance along with the best possible combination of quality, quantity, and size of stones.

Only a diamond can cut a diamond. This fact is demonstrated at all stages in the production of a faceted stone: sawing or cleaving, shaping, and polishing. Each of these steps is complicated by two factors: the inherent hardness of the diamond and the "grain" of the rough stone. This grain is so resistant that neither saw nor cleaver can make progress against it. Thus, the stone must be studied carefully to determine which way the grain runs before it may be cut.

If the rough is to be sawed, a paper-thin phosphor-bronze disc charged with diamond dust is used. Sawing is a painstaking process that may require anywhere from one week to several months. The alternative to sawing—cleaving—is much more dramatic—and more dangerous. The rough stone is always studied carefully to calculate the direction of the cleavage plane. Once this is determined, a small V-shaped groove is placed on the stone to help guide the heavy steel cleavage blade. With proper calculations and preparation, one quick, strong blow of a mallet cleaves the rough neatly in two. The slightest error in calculation, in the direction of the wedge, or in the delivery of the blow could shatter the stone. Therein lies the great risk inherent in cleaving. The cleaving of such major stones as the Jonker, the Vargas, the Liberator, and the Star of Sierra Leone is truly awe-inspiring.

Once the primary divisions are made by sawing or cleaving, each individual stone is shaped by rubbing it against another diamond on a lathe-like machine called a girdler. After the final form is roughed out, the diamond is faceted and then polished by pressing it against an iron wheel that is coated with diamond dust. Virtually every diamond emerges from this operation with fifty-eight facets. Each facet is a definite, relative size and is placed at a specific, predetermined angle in order to provide the best proportions for maximum light refraction within the stone. This careful, geometric faceting is what gives the stone its sparkle and brilliance.

The complexity of all the factors that must be taken into consideration in the production of a single diamond is astounding.

Even more remarkable is the fact that Harry Winston was responsible for the creation of more than seventy-five diamonds weighing over 30 carats, many of which are D-flawless.

What follows, then, represents only a portion of the most remarkable collection of stones ever assembled. No king, nawab, or emperor ever possessed more diamond treasure in his life.

The 44-carat Qamar-I-Saltana diamond.

ARCOTS

In 1751, Robert Clive, an officer in the employ of the British East India Company, captured and successfully defended the city of Arcot, in southern India, against overwhelming odds. Clive was knighted by King George III of England for his part in this crucial battle, which was a determining factor in the exclusion of other European powers from India. The local rulers then became vassals of the crown. In 1777, one of them, Nawab Azim-Ud-Daula of Arcot, thought it a fitting gesture to give the royal consort of King George III, Queen Charlotte, five large diamonds.[2] The history of two of these five diamonds can be traced to the present day: the two pear shapes, weighing a total of 57.35 carats, that Queen Charlotte had set as earrings and that historically have been referred to as the Arcots.

Queen Charlotte loved the diamonds given to her by the Nawab of Arcot, and wore them often. Since it was impossible to divide them equitably among her four daughters, she left specific instructions in her will that the diamonds were to be sold and the money distributed equally among the four. After her death in 1818, the Arcots, as well as the other three stones, were sold to the then crown jewelers, Rundell, Bridge & Company.

At that time, it was the custom of the royal family to borrow diamonds and precious stones from the crown jewelers for important state functions. In 1831, Rundell, Bridge set the Arcots in a crown they created for Queen Adelaide, the consort of King William IV, to wear at his coronation. The stones had been returned to the crown jewelers sometime before the death of John

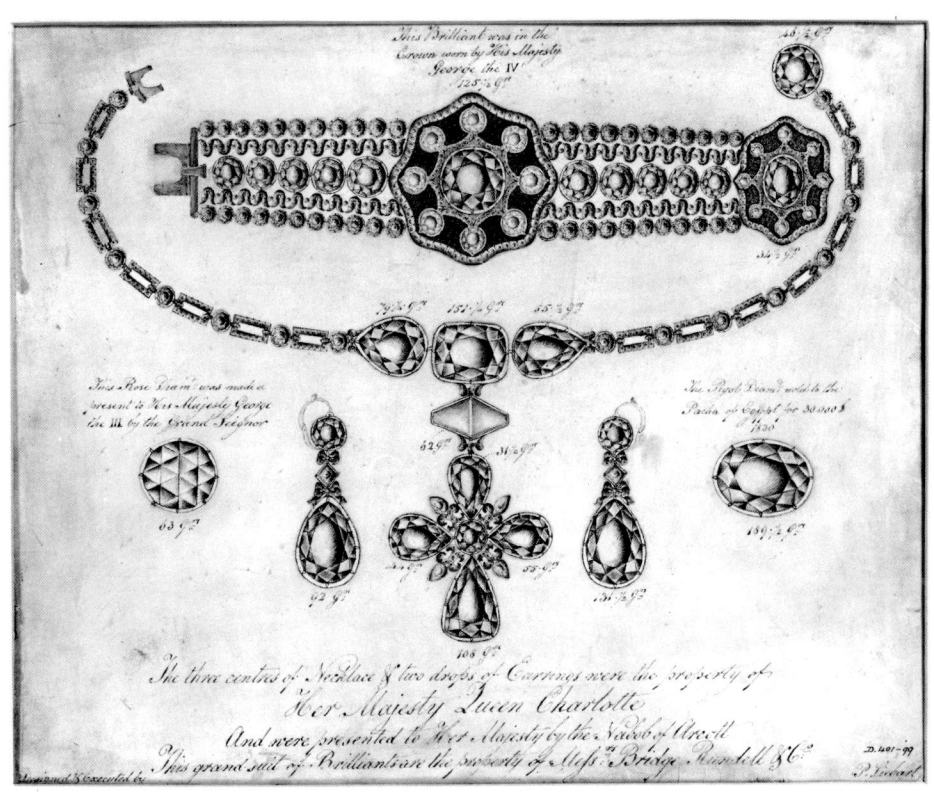

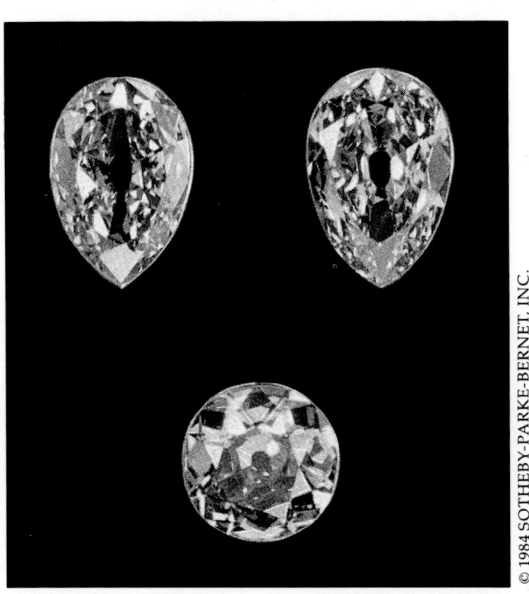

TOP CENTER: *The two Arcot diamonds appear in this 19th-century lithograph set as earrings. The center stone in the bracelet is the King George IV diamond.*

TOP: *The Arcot diamonds and the King George IV.*

RIGHT: *The Arcots as prepared for Queen Adelaide of England in 1831.*

The Westminster tiara as worn by the Duchess of Westminster in 1931.

Bridge in 1834 which led to the closure of the firm. As part of the sale of the company, an auction was held in 1837 which featured two other historical stones—the King George IV and the Nassak—as well as the Arcots. The Duke of Westminster purchased all four of these stones as a birthday present for his wife.

In 1930, the Arcots were mounted in the family headpiece, the Westminster tiara, together with 1,421 smaller diamonds and the 32-carat King George IV diamond. In June 1959, the then Duke of Westminster, beset by heavy inheritance taxes, decided to sell the tiara. It was purchased by Harry Winston for $308,000—one of the largest single-item jewelry sales up to that time.

When the Arcots were removed from the tiara and the bezel setting that surrounded them, it was discovered that they were not the matched pair that their history had previously portrayed: one weighed 33.70 carats and the other 23.65 carats. Mr. Winston recut both stones for greater clarity and brilliance: the larger to a flawless 31.01 carats, and its smaller mate to 18.85 carats. Each was mounted as a ring and sold to American clients in 1959 and 1960, respectively. The elaborate tiara minus its famous diamonds was purchased by a client from Texas in 1977.

PHOTOGRAPH BY CECIL BEATON. COURTESY VOGUE. © 1931 (RENEWED 1959) THE CONDÉ NAST PUBLICATIONS, INC.

ANASTASIA

In 1972, Harry Winston purchased a rough diamond weighing 307.30 carats. It was then fashioned into three D-flawless emerald-cut diamonds of 43.95 carats, 30.90 carats, and 22.88 carats, respectively, all of which were sold as rings that same year.

The largest stone was named in honor of the daughter of the last Czar of Russia, Anastasia Nicholayevna, who is rumored to have escaped the executioners who killed her parents and siblings in 1918. This stone was stolen during the owner's visit to Paris in 1982. The thieves were later apprehended, however, and the diamond was recovered intact.

ASHOKA

This 41.37-carat D-flawless diamond of unknown antiquity was named in honor of Ashoka Maurya (268–233 B.C.), the Buddhist warrior-emperor who ruled the greatest empire in the history of the Indian subcontinent.

This diamond, like so many other famous stones, had its origin in the Golconda region (now Hyderabad) in southern India. From approximately 1000 A.D. until the discovery of diamonds in Brazil in 1725, the ancient alluvial fields of Golconda yielded most of the world's finest and most famous diamonds.

The shape of the stone is rather unusual, a modified cushion antique cut. This is an older form of the brilliant cut, and has a rectangular girdle outline with rounded corners. Mr. Winston first purchased the Ashoka from an Indian dealer in 1947; he subsequently sold and repurchased it several times. In 1977, the stone was recut from its original weight of 42.47 carats before it was sold again as a ring.

BRIOLETTE

This South African diamond is considered one of the truly unique gems in the world today, not only because of its D color at 90.38 carats, but also because of its unusual shape. The stone is cut in the rarely seen briolette style: the entire surface of this large drop is covered by hundreds of tiny symmetrically placed triangular facets.

Although legend has dated the stone back as far as Eleanor of Aquitaine, in the twelfth century, research for this book revealed that the stone was actually cut in Neuilly, France, in 1908–1909 at the then-famous diamond cutters of Atanik Eknayan. The briolette cut was chosen because it best accommodated the odd shape of the original piece of rough. American philanthropist George Blumenthal purchased the stone from Cartier in Paris in 1910. In 1946, Harry Winston obtained the diamond from Mrs. R. K. Robertson, Blumenthal's widow.

The Briolette was sold in 1947 to an Indian maharaja. At that time, it was mounted in such a way that it could be worn as a pendant to a necklace, as a clip, or as a diadem to rest on the forehead of a harem favorite while a diamond bandeau held it firmly in place. Mr. Winston repurchased the stone in 1956 at the death of the maharaja. He had it remounted as a pendant to a V-shaped necklace that contained 157 marquise diamonds and subsequently sold it to Mrs. I. W. Killam of Canada. Following Mrs. Killam's death in 1967, Mr. Winston purchased her entire jewelry collection. In 1971, the Briolette was sold to an important titled European family.

CORNFLOWER BLUE

In 1958, Harry Winston purchased a rough South African diamond weighing 158 carats. Two stones, both a striking blue, were cut from it: a 31.92-carat flawless pear shape and a 12.39-carat flawless round brilliant. The larger diamond was christened the Cornflower Blue, and was sold in 1969 mounted as a pendant to a necklace. Harry Winston repurchased the stone two years later and then sold it to a client in the Middle East. The round brilliant was set as a ring and sold in 1969.

CROWN OF CHARLEMAGNE

A flawless round sky-blue diamond that originally weighed 42.50 carats was purchased by Harry Winston from a Spanish client in 1949. It was believed to have been set in one of the crowns of Emperor Charlemagne—an unlikely but nevertheless romantic legend. Mr. Winston had the stone recut and mounted as a pin for Mrs. I. W. Killam of Canada. He repurchased the diamond in 1967 following Mrs. Killam's death. The stone was recut slightly to 37.05 carats and then sold in 1968.

COUNTESS SZÉCHÉNYI

In January 1908, Gladys Moore Vanderbilt, the youngest of the seven children of Cornelius Vanderbilt and the former Alice Claypoole Gwynne, was married to Count László Széchényi. Gladys Vanderbilt was a great-granddaughter of Commodore Cornelius Vanderbilt, a transportation magnate who was reportedly the richest man in America at the time of his death in 1877. Count Széchényi, from an ancient Hungarian family, was a chamberlain to Emperor Franz Joseph II of the Austro-Hungarian Empire. The count subsequently had a distinguished career as Hungary's minister, first to Washington and then to London, between World War I and his death in 1938. Although Countess Széchényi was involved in many philanthropic endeavors, she is best remembered for her gift in 1948 to the city of Newport, Rhode Island: the lease, for one dollar a year, of her family home, the Breakers, a fifty-two-room "cottage" built in 1895 by her father.

As a wedding present, Alice Gwynne Vanderbilt presented her daughter with a magnificent diamond tiara befitting her new position in the court of the Hapsburgs in Budapest and Vienna. The center stone of the tiara was a detachable pear-shaped diamond weighing 62.05 carats. No information is available on the history of the diamond before it was purchased by Mrs. Vanderbilt. Countess Széchényi wore the diamond on a necklace

Countess Széchényi, as she appeared at the coronation of King Charles IV of Hungary in 1916, wears as a necklace the 62.05- carat diamond that now bears her name.

with the tiara at the coronation of King Charles IV of Hungary in 1916.

In 1959, Countess Széchényi sold the large diamond to Harry Winston. The D-color stone was recut to a flawless 59.38 carats. The stone was mounted as a pendant to a V-shaped necklace that contained over 42 carats of marquise, round, and pear-shaped diamonds. The necklace was sold to an American industrialist in 1966.

The Countess Széchényi diamond as sold in 1966. The accompanying pear-shaped diamonds weigh a total of 42 carats.

DEEPDENE

This 104.88-carat cushion-cut yellow diamond was displayed at the Philadelphia Academy of Sciences during the 1930s and 1940s. It was loaned to that museum by Cary W. Bok, of the founding family of Curtis Publications, and had been named after Mrs. Bok's family estate. In 1954, Harry Winston purchased the diamond from Mr. Bok and had it mounted in a clip surrounded by thirteen diamonds weighing a total of 18 carats. The Deepdene was sold in 1955 to Mrs. Eleanor Loder of Canada.

In 1971, a 104.52-carat yellow diamond that was said to have been the Deepdene was put up for auction at Christie's in Geneva.

DEAL SWEETENER

In 1974, Harry Winston and Harry Oppenheimer, head of De Beers Consolidated Mines, Ltd., concluded an agreement whereby Harry Winston would purchase a parcel of rough diamonds for $24,500,000. The transaction—the largest individual sale of diamonds in history—took less than a minute. When Mr. Winston asked Mr. Oppenheimer, "How about a little something to sweeten the deal?" Harry Oppenheimer pulled a 181-carat rough diamond out of his pocket and rolled it across the table. Harry Winston picked the stone up, smiled, and said simply, "Thanks."

This piece of rough was cut into five gem diamonds. The largest, a 45.31-carat D-flawless emerald cut, was aptly christened the Deal Sweetener. The others were an emerald cut of 24.67 carats and three pear shapes of 10.80 carats, 4.19 carats, and 1.45 carats, respectively. All five stones were sold that same year.

EUGÉNIE BLUE

Like the Briolette, this 31-carat sapphire blue heart-shaped diamond was cut by the firm Atanik Eknayan in Neuilly, France, shortly before Cartier sold it to an important Argentine family in 1910. At various times since then it has also been known as the Blue Heart diamond. The name Eugénie Blue came because at one time it was rumored—falsely, of course— to have been associated with the Empress Eugénie of France. It appeared in Paris again in 1953, and was purchased by an important European titled family. In 1959, Harry Winston acquired the stone. Mounted as a ring, it was sold in 1964 to Mrs. Marjorie Merriweather Post, who subsequently donated it to the Smithsonian Institution.

ÉTOILE DU DÉSERT

This 50.67-carat D-color pear-shaped stone was acquired by Harry Winston in 1977 and mounted as the center stone in the pendant to a fabulous diamond necklace that was sold that same year to a Saudi Arabian prince. The pendant also contained forty smaller pear-shaped diamonds, weighing a total of 42 carats. A 16-carat D-flawless marquise was among the other fine stones in the necklace. The total diamond weight in this remarkable piece was more than 250 carats.

HOPE

This 45.52-carat dark blue stone is undoubtedly one of the world's most famous diamonds, with a history heavily veiled by superstition. Most importantly, the story of the Hope is both more complete and more complex than that of any other diamond in the world. Over the years, it has developed into a fascinating mix of legend and fact. While legend is the only basis for much of the aura of notoriety that surrounds the Hope, many of the known facts lend their own touch of tragedy.

The legend first unfolds in 1642 in southwest India, where Jean-Baptiste Tavernier, French adventurer and gem merchant, was shown a rough blue diamond that is believed originally to have weighed 112.50 carats. At that time, any diamond over 10 carats became, by law, the property of the local prince. It is not known how this stone was smuggled out of India, but it eventually appeared as one of the many large diamonds that Tavernier sold to Louis XIV (the "Sun King") in 1668. Within a few years, though, Tavernier's son had squandered the fortune his father had received for the jewels, and the old man, at 80, returned to India in quest of new wealth; reportedly his quest ended tragically, as he was torn apart and eaten by wild dogs.

Louis XIV ordered the cutting of the stone, now called the French Blue diamond; the result was a 67.50-carat pear shape, which remained part of the French Crown Jewels for over 124 years. According to the legend, Louis XIV wore the French Blue only once, and died shortly thereafter from smallpox. Louis XV is said never to have worn it, but to have loaned it to one of his mistresses, Countess DuBarry, who was beheaded during the French

Revolution. It is also said that Louis XVI thought it the most beautiful diamond in the world and that his queen, the ill-fated Marie Antoinette, wore it often. The Princess de Lamballe, devoted friend of Marie Antoinette, also was reported to have worn it; she was cruelly murdered by a Paris mob during the revolution.

On September 17, 1792, the entire collection of Crown Jewels was stolen from the treasury building in Paris. Some of the royal diamonds were later recovered, but not the French Blue.

The whereabouts of the diamond during the twenty years that followed have never been confirmed. During this period, however, the French Blue diamond was said to have been recut by Wilhelm Fals, a Dutch diamond cutter. Fals's son, Hendrick, reportedly stole the gem from his father, who died of grief from his son's betrayal. Overcome with remorse, Hendrick committed suicide.

The recut French Blue then surfaced in London in 1830, where it was sold to Henry Phillip Hope for about $90,000. According to some accounts, Hope and his descendants were beset with tragedy. The last heir to the Hope fortune, Lord Francis Pelham Clinton Hope, was plagued by severe financial problems, and his first wife, American stage actress May Yohe, deserted him for another man after her unsuccessful attempt to make a stage comeback.

The next turn of the story places the Hope in the possession of Sir Caspar Purdon-Clarke, a well-known antiquarian of the time. He claimed that an old man came to him with a parcel of dirty jewelry he had bought at a sheriff's auction in Brighton, England. The jewels had been discovered in the room of a music hall actress, who had quit her shabby lodgings along with her husband, leaving a pile of debts in their wake. Sir Caspar instantly recognized the Hope, as well as several other pieces from the Hope estate, and immediately turned the stones over to the Hope family trustees.

In 1901, the trustees convinced the courts to break the life interest clause regarding the Hope and the other estate jewels so that they could be sold to reduce Lord Francis's debts. Supposedly, the Hope was then purchased by a New York jeweler—whose firm went bankrupt a few years after the diamond arrived. The next owner was a French broker named Jacques Colot, who was said to have gone mad and committed suicide after he sold the Hope to Prince Ivan Kanitovski, a Russian. Prince Kanitovski was somewhat of a bon-vivant in Paris, but friends said that after he bought the stone, he turned morose. The legend continues that the prince loaned the jewel to actress Lorens Ladue, of the Folies Bergères, and (out of jealousy) shot her from a spectator's box on the first night she wore it. He himself was murdered by revolutionaries a few days afterward.[3]

The next owner reportedly was a rich Egyptian merchant, Habib Bey, who drowned along with his whole family in a steamer collision off Singapore. At first it was thought that the diamond had gone down with the ship, but it turned up in the possession of a Greek broker, Simon Montharides.[4]

In 1908, the story continues, the diamond was purchased from Simon Montharides by Sultan Abdul Hamid II of the Ottoman Empire (now Turkey). After selling the stone, Montharides was thrown over a precipice while motoring with his wife and child, and all were killed. In Turkey, it was worn by the sultan's harem favorite, Salama Zubaya, who was later executed by her master.[5]

After his purchase of the Hope, Abdul Hamid, sensing that revolution was imminent, reportedly decided to have a nest egg waiting for him in France. He schemed with a trusted minister, the Grand Azize, to smuggle out several large stones, including the Hope. The Grand Azize secretly plotted to sell the jewels in France and enjoy the proceeds himself. For this nefarious scheme, he engaged the services of a young Turk, who proved to be just as unscrupulous as the sultan and his minister. En route to France, the messenger carefully hid the jewels in a remote corner of the train. He then shot himself in the cheek, creating a great commotion, as he alternately shouted and wept about his "stolen" jewels. When the excitement subsided, he took the jewels and secreted them about his person.

There seem to be two versions of what happened next. One is that the young double agent disposed of the jewels in France at the monts-de-piété (pawn shops), for a princely sum. The other is that the young man, posing as an agent of the Young Turks Party, sold the stones directly to a Mr. Selim Habib, who exhibited them for sale in Paris in June of 1909 under the name "Collection Habib." It was said that in November of 1909, Habib went down with the French liner, Le Seyne, in Rhio Straits near Singapore. Whichever story is true, the sultan reportedly dispatched his dreaded secret police to bring back the thief, who spent the rest of his days haunted by the fear of imminent capture. In the late 1940s, still living in a remote corner of France, he never ventured anywhere without bodyguards. Sultan Abdul Hamid was deposed and subsequently exiled in the Young Turks revolution of 1909; he never received one penny from the sale of the diamonds.

The legend surrounding the Hope before it was purchased in 1910 by Pierre Cartier has appeared in a variety of publications throughout the world, embellished with each new account. In the past, little attempt was made to verify the confusing and often contradictory stories about the stone. Indeed, the few who challenged the legend soon discovered that even basic facts about the stone, such as its exact size and weight, were scarce. Recently, however, a number of people have attempted to cleave fact from fiction to reveal the true origin and early history of the great blue stone.

Most notable is Susanne Steinem Patch, who in her 1976 book, *Blue Mystery: The Story of the Hope Diamond*,[6] investigates the legend of the curse, and concludes that much of the lore surrounding the famous blue stone cannot be substantiated. According to Patch, Tavernier probably did bring the large blue rough diamond with him from India and did sell it to King Louis XIV. Around 1686, Tavernier sold his land and the barony of Aubonne on the promise of becoming an ambassador to India. When the plans fell through, he traveled to Europe and died of unknown causes in Moscow at age 84. The first known account that Tavernier was killed by wild dogs seems to have been given by Pierre Cartier when he showed the stone to its prospective owner, Evalyn Walsh McLean.

King Louis XIV did not die of smallpox, but of gangrene. It is unlikely that either Marie Antoinette or her friend, the Princess de Lamballe, ever wore the stone, as it was set in the famous Order of the Golden Fleece in 1749 (the year of de Lamballe's birth) and was worn exclusively by King Louis XVI until he was deposed. It is true that de Lamballe was killed by a mob in Paris during the revolution, and both King Louis XVI and Marie Antoinette were indeed beheaded. During the chaos of the revolution, the French Blue was stolen from the State Treasury in 1792.

An oval blue diamond weighing 45.52 carats appeared in England in 1812. Gem experts agree that it was cut from the original French Blue, but there is no evidence that the supposed cutter Wilhelm Fals ever existed. Eliason did sell the stone to Henry

Phillip Hope, a London banker, who, from all accounts, led a normal life. A bachelor, he left the stone to his oldest nephew, Henry Thomas Hope, the eighth Duke of Newcastle, who died at the age of 54. His widow died in 1887, having bequeathed the blue diamond to her grandson, Lord Francis Pelham Clinton (the son of her daughter), on the condition that he thereafter call himself Lord Francis Pelham Clinton Hope. In 1894, Lord Francis Hope married May Yohe, an American actress, who often wore the famous blue diamond and later had a glass model of it made for a stage comeback, which did not prove successful. In 1901, May left Lord Francis for another man. Her next husband was later murdered, and a hotel she built burned to the ground. She died in Boston in 1938, her only income being a $16.50-per-week W.P.A.* job.

Lord Francis's notorious financial difficulties seemed to have been directly related to his own personal folly—for the most part his passion for gambling. He tried several times to sell the Hope to pay off his debts, but was prevented from doing so by the courts, as the diamond was a life interest only. He was bankrupt by 1895. In 1901, he finally obtained permission to sell the stone. At age sixty-two, however, he inherited the title and the property of the Duke of Newcastle from his older brother. He died in comfort at age seventy-five, leaving his title and the estate to his son.

There is no evidence to support the Colot story. Likewise, the story of Prince Kanitovski's murder of a young actress and his own violent death shortly thereafter are, according to Patch, unfounded.

---

*W.P.A. is the acronym for Work Projects Administration, a U.S. Government-funded program set up during the Depression years to create jobs.

In reality, Lord Francis Hope sold the stone to diamond merchant Simon Frankel of New York. In 1908, Frankel sold the Hope to Selim Habib, a Turkish diamond collector, of Paris, who was indeed killed in the steamer collision off Singapore.[7] It was "reliably reported" at the time that Habib had acted as an agent for Sultan Abdul Hamid II when Habib purchased the stone.[8] In 1909, the *New York Times* reported that the stone had been sold to French diamond expert Louis Aucoc, for one of his clients.[9] The Cartier firm in Paris bought the Hope from a jeweler named Rosenau.

In 1910, Pierre Cartier showed the stone to a young couple, Mr. and Mrs. Edward B. McLean, in Paris. Mr. McLean's family owned the *Washington Post* and other important newspapers, and Mrs. McLean's father had discovered the lucrative Camp Bird gold mine in Colorado.

Mrs. McLean had a consuming passion for jewels; as she later wrote in her autobiography, "they make me feel comfortable and even happy. The truth is, when I neglect to wear jewels, astute members of my family call in doctors because it is a sign I'm becoming ill." (Two years prior to being shown the Hope, while on a honeymoon visit to Paris, she had purchased the 94.80-carat Star of the East.) When Mrs. McLean first saw the Hope in the summer of 1910, she rejected it with the simple explanation, "I don't like the setting." But in November of 1910, Pierre Cartier again showed her the diamond, now reset, this time at her home in Washington, D.C. After keeping it for the weekend, she decided she had to have it. Despite the legends, of which she was well aware (and which she even relished), Mrs. McLean purchased the stone in 1911. In later years, she said that she felt herself immune from any evil that might accompany the diamond, but she "wouldn't let my friends or children touch it." She said she received "letter after letter from May Yohe, now trying to recoup

LEFT: *Evalyn Walsh McLean wearing the Star of the East on a diamond bandeau around her head and the Hope diamond at her neck.*

RIGHT: *Mrs. McLean often wore the Hope and the Star of the East together on the same necklace.*

some bit of happiness from the ruin of her life. She blamed the diamond; and as one woman to another, she begged me to throw it away and break its spell."[10]

Mrs. McLean became a leader of Washington society, famed as a hostess at whose gala parties presidents, cabinet ministers, and ambassadors gathered. The Hope diamond, worn high on the celebrated lady's neck, invariably stole the limelight from her nationally and internationally famous guests. She often wore the Hope and the Star of the East on the same necklace, one beneath the other. When not wearing them, she kept them in her favorite hiding place: the cushions of her sofa.

Despite all the glamour and gaiety, luxury and power, Mrs. McLean's personal life had many tragic chapters. Her nine-year-old son, Vinson, protected by his parents almost fanatically, slipped away from his guards in 1918 and was hit by a car and killed. Her husband was implicated in the Teapot Dome Scandal of the 1920s. He divorced his famous wife in 1929, and eventually became mentally unbalanced. He died in an institution in 1946.

In speaking of the diamond, Evalyn Walsh McLean said, "I like to pretend the thing brings good luck. I kid myself, of course—as a matter of fact, the luckiest thing about it is that, if I ever had to, I could hock it."[11] The vast family fortune shrank away several times, and the Hope diamond was often used as collateral for loans.

In fact, on one occasion when she traveled to her loan company in downtown New York to reclaim her jewels, she merely stuffed them into her dress, and casually walked unescorted into the busy street. The company employees were aghast at her lack of precaution. She then went uptown to a luncheon over which she lingered too long. As Mrs. McLean ended the tale in a nonchalant and almost blasé manner, "we jumped into a taxi, and then ran through the station so fast I thought I would be shaking the stones out of my bosom at every step."[12]

Evalyn Walsh McLean wore the Hope everywhere: to the movies, to distribute sandwiches to veterans of the first World War, and even on the streets of Moscow. But she continued to be haunted by the tragedy that so many had claimed lay with the diamond. Mrs. McLean died of pneumonia on April 26, 1947, only a few months after her twenty-five-year-old daughter had died from an overdose of sleeping tablets. Mrs. McLean left instructions in her will that the Hope was to be put away in a bank vault for twenty years. At that time, it was to be sold, cut up, or divided among her seven grandchildren. The trustees and the Surrogate Court in Washington found this provision of the will impractical and determined that it was in the best interest of the estate to sell the Hope together with the seventy-three other pieces of her jewelry. Harry Winston purchased the collection in April of 1949 for over one million dollars. In addition to the Hope and the Star of the East, some of the highlights of her collection included the 15-carat Star of the South diamond, the 31-carat McLean diamond, and a clip with a 9-carat green emerald-cut diamond.

To give the public an opportunity to see the infamous Hope, Mr. Winston used the stone as the central attraction in his Court of Jewels, which toured the United States from 1949 to 1953. Until 1958, the Hope was used at many such exhibits and charitable functions.

Mr. Winston demonstrated little concern about the infamy that surrounded the Hope diamond. He said that owning the diamond gave him nothing but pleasure and good fortune, and blithely carried it with him across the Atlantic on several occasions. However, he did enjoy recounting the following story about his personal experience with the legend of the Hope:

> "A few years ago I traveled to Lisbon with my wife. Since our two sons were quite young at the time, we decided to return home on separate planes, as people with children often do. It was arranged that my wife would leave Lisbon for New York on Friday evening, and that I would take a plane on the following day. My wife's plane took off on schedule, and landed at Santa Maria (in the Azores) for the usual refueling. There some slight engine trouble caused a delay of two or three hours. While waiting for repairs to be done, the passengers chatted among themselves, and the fact that Mrs. Harry Winston was on the plane was soon known to all. One man went so far as to refuse to continue the journey and asked to be booked on the next plane.

"On the way to the airport the next day I was handed a cablegram from my wife announcing her safe arrival, which I hastily crammed into my pocket with other papers. Climbing aboard the plane, I took a sedative and settled down, glad to notice that the adjacent seat was vacant and I could sleep in peace. I awoke from a pleasant nap when we touched down at Santa Maria to refuel, and got out to stretch my legs for awhile.

"When we reboarded the plane to take off for New York, I found that the vacant seat was now occupied. Its occupant was bubbling over with a story about his escape from traveling on the same plane as the wife of the owner of the Hope diamond.

"'I'm not superstitious,' he said, 'but why should I tempt fate? I decided then and there to change planes and here I am, safe and sound.' He talked animatedly for some time, but eventually grew quiet enough for me to drop off to sleep again. Then his voice broke in on my slumber: 'I wonder if that plane arrived safely?'

"I couldn't resist it. I fished the cablegram from my pocket and handed it to him, saying nothing. He gazed dumbly at me, and didn't open his mouth again that night."[13]

In 1958, Harry Winston donated the Hope diamond to the Smithsonian Institution as a gift to the American people. The Smithsonian still receives several letters a year blaming the nation's ills on the "cursed" diamond and begging the museum to somehow get rid of it. Curse notwithstanding, the Hope is certainly one of the most beautiful, enigmatic diamonds ever to grace a royal scepter, a harem favorite, or the neck of a beautiful woman.

IDOL'S EYE

The recorded history of this 70.20-carat flawless oval diamond traces the stone back to the early part of the seventeenth century, when it was found in India's Golconda region. In 1607, the East India Company seized the stone from its owner, a Persian prince named Rahab, as payment for his debts.

The stone then disappeared from public record for almost 300 years. In 1906, it was said to have been rediscovered in the possession of Sultan Abdul Hamid II of the Ottoman Empire. In deference to a legend (however improbable) that it had once been used as the eye of a sacred idol in the Temple of Benhazi (the Ottomans, for the most part Muslim, were not allowed to worship idols or statues), the stone was called the Idol's Eye.

Although virtually nothing has been written about the travels of the stone during the three centuries after the East India Company claimed it from Prince Rahab, two stories in particular have followed the Idol's Eye to the present. According to one, the diamond came into the possession of the Ottomans many years ago, reportedly part of the plunder from their invasion of central Asia. Another is that one of Abdul Hamid's predecessors had recklessly abducted the beautiful Princess Rasheetah from her lover, the Sultan of Kashmir. The Idol's Eye, the sultan's most treasured possession, was used as ransom for the safe return of the princess.

Just prior to what has become known as the Young Turks revolt of 1909, the Idol's Eye (together with the Hope and the Star of the East) appeared in Paris. According to the second much-published story, it was originally intended to provide a comfortable

retirement for the sultan, who anticipated a hasty retreat from the throne. Instead, the three stones were stolen by his messenger and sold to French pawnshops.

We do know that the Idol's Eye appeared at the June 1909 auction held in Paris by gem connoisseur Selim Habib. It was subsequently purchased by a Spanish nobleman, then came into the possession of a London bank, and eventually was obtained by a Dutch diamond dealer, from whom Harry Winston purchased the stone in November of 1946 (in a whirlwind deal that took him from New York to London and back before others were even aware that the stone had been offered for sale).

In 1947, Mr. Winston sold the Idol's Eye to Mrs. May Bonfils Stanton, daughter of the publisher and co-founder of the *Denver Post*. At that time it was mounted as the center stone in a necklace that included eighty-six other diamonds which weighed a total of 35 carats. In 1962, after the death of Mrs. Stanton, the Idol's Eye was sold at auction in New York City.

INDORE PEAR SHAPES

In 1926, His Highness Tukoji Rao III, the Holkar Maharaja of Indore, India, was forced to abdicate in favor of his seventeen-year-old son because of a scandal concerning the maharaja's favorite dancing girl, Mumtaz Begum. When His Highness Tukoji Rao III abdicated, he retained his immense personal fortune, which included two pear-shaped Golconda diamonds that weighed 46.95 carats and 46.70 carats, respectively.

While traveling in Switzerland, the former maharaja met Nancy Anne Miller, a wealthy young American from Seattle, Washington (her father had discovered gold in 1898 at Miller Gulch near Valdez, Alaska). The two were married in 1928 amid much international publicity. The former Miss Miller, who had entered the Hindu religion in preparation for her marriage, was subsequently known as the Maharanee Shamista Devi Holkar.

In 1946, Harry Winston purchased the two diamond drops that the former maharaja and his American wife had both worn on many occasions. The two stones were recut to 44.62 and 44.18 carats, respectively, and were added to Mr. Winston's famous Court of Jewels exhibit. In 1953, Mr. Winston sold the Indore Pear Shapes to a client from Philadelphia; in 1958, he repurchased the stones and sold them to a New York client. In 1976, Mr. Winston purchased the Indore Pear Shapes once again and subsequently sold them to a member of a royal family. Most recently, in 1981, the two famous diamonds were sold at auction in Geneva, Switzerland.

JONKER

In January 1934, a 726-carat diamond was found in an alluvial deposit on the farm of Jacobus Jonker at Elandsfontein, near Pretoria, South Africa. The stone, the seventh largest rough diamond on record, was of unusually fine color and purity. In 1935, Harry Winston purchased it in London from the Diamond Producers Association. After much concern and debate over the safest way to get the diamond to New York, Mr. Winston decided to send it via regular mail, registered, for sixty-four cents postage!

Child star Shirley Temple holds the 726-carat rough Jonker diamond.

The largest stone cut from the Jonker rough weighs 125.35 carats and is now known as the Jonker diamond.

The Jonker diamond represented the first time such a major stone was ever cleaved in the United States. The largest diamond fashioned from the rough was a sixty-six facet emerald cut that originally weighed 142.90 carats; it was recut in 1937 to 125.35 carats with fifty-eight facets, to give it a more oblong outline. Because Mr. Winston loved this stone, which he christened the Jonker diamond, for many years he refused to sell it, using it instead for display at various charitable exhibitions. Not until 1951 did Mr. Winston part with the Jonker, allowing it to be sold to King Farouk of Egypt. After Farouk went into exile in 1952, nothing was heard of the stone until 1959, when it was rumored that Queen Ratna of Nepal had been seen wearing it. It has since been confirmed that the late Farouk did sell the diamond to the tiny Himalayan country for a reputed price of one hundred thousand dollars. In 1974, the Jonker was sold at auction in Hong Kong for four million dollars.

From the remaining rough, a marquise and ten emerald cuts were fashioned. The larger gems included emerald cuts of 41.30 carats, 35.45 carats, 30.70 carats, 25.66 carats, and 24.41 carats. The 30.70-carat and 24.41-carat stones were sold to American clients; the other three stones were sold to Indian maharajas. The smallest of the eleven stones, a 5.30-carat emerald cut, was auctioned in New York City in October 1975.

Winston's cutting of the Jonker is a story in itself, especially as recounted by Harmon and Elsie Tupper:

> In 1935 Winston startled the gem experts on both sides of the Atlantic by snapping up, at the neat price of $800,000, the huge Jonker rough diamond shortly after its discovery by an obscure South African farmer. Weighing 726 carats, or 1,452 times the weight of the average engagement-ring diamond, the jewel was the largest to come to light since the great Cullinan find of 1905. It was also shaped in such a way as to make successful cutting a fifty-fifty gamble at best. Staid lapidarians recalled the unfortunate cleavage of the Cullinan, now in the English crown, when two thirds of the precious mineral were lost in waste. At that rate, they figured complacently, Winston would be out more than half a million on his investment. But their calculations did not include Harry's enormous patience and the vast store of lapidary knowledge behind his shrewd brown eyes.
>
> For fourteen long months he studied the Jonker. Day after day he plotted different cutting combinations and experimented with innumerable glass casts that simulated the rough jewel's grain and

crystalline structure. Even with these elaborate preparations, luck was still such an important factor that Lloyd's of London turned down Winston's request for $200,000 insurance against damage.

His nerve was put to the test on a July day in 1936 when he suddenly ordered his chief diamond cleaver to split the gem. One crisp tap and the job was done. An invisible "knot" or other flaw could have shattered the Jonker to bits and all but ruined Winston.

But his months of study, plus his Lady Luck, paid off. The perfectly cleaved stone was cut into twelve diamonds. The largest jewel, the Jonker No. 1, which he kept for himself, weighed 125.35 carats, almost triple the size of Evalyn Walsh McLean's Hope bauble, and flashed with dazzling brilliance from a platinum necklace set with 110 baguettes.[14]

KING GEORGE IV

In 1821, the then crown jewelers, Rundell, Bridge & Company, were commissioned to create a new crown for the coronation of King George IV of England. The principal stone was a 32.23-carat round diamond. Although in his book, *History of the Crown Jewels of Europe,* Lord Twining traces the story of this diamond from 1821 to contemporary times,[15] he offers no information on its history prior to 1821.

According to Lord Twining, the crown jewelers often loaned royalty diamonds or colored stones for special occasions. King George IV was billed £6,525 by Rundell, Bridge for the three-year loan of the diamonds in the crown he ordered. Lord Twining quotes an account given at the time that "the crown made for this occasion was really a magnificent one. Very many remarkable fine ornaments were introduced into it, the principal one being a very fine round stone of the diameter of a shilling. . . . It was cut in the truest style and its proportions were mathematically correct."[16] After the coronation, the diamond was returned to the crown jewelers and was displayed in an elaborate diamond bracelet (pictured in the lithograph at the top of page 43).

In 1831, Queen Adelaide commissioned Rundell, Bridge to create a crown for her to wear at the coronation of her husband, King William IV, George IV's younger brother. Into this crown were placed the King George IV diamond as well as the two large pear-shaped diamonds known as the Arcots.

The diamonds were returned to Rundell, Bridge after the coronation; they remained there until 1834, when the business was

The Westminster tiara, with the King George IV diamond as the center stone and the Arcot diamonds on either side.

closed following the death of John Bridge. In 1837, as part of the sale of the company, the King George IV was offered at auction together with the famous Nassak and Arcot diamonds. The Duke of Westminster purchased all four stones. In 1930, the then Duke of Westminster had the King George IV set as the center ornament of the elaborate Westminster tiara, in which the Arcots were also featured. The tiara was borrowed on many occasions by members of the royal family. The center section could also be detached and worn separately as a "corsage ornament" (an elaborate jeweled pin worn in place of or in addition to a corsage, popular during the fifty years prior to World War I). In 1959, the Westminster family was forced to sell the tiara to help cover inheritance taxes. It was purchased by Harry Winston for $308,000 — one of the largest single-item jewelry sales up to that time.

When the King George IV was removed from its setting, it was determined that, contrary to earlier reports, the stone had not been cut to achieve its full potential. Harry Winston had the stone recut to 26.77 carats for greater brilliance. Set as a ring, it was sold in 1959 to an American client. On December 9, 1970, it was auctioned in New York.

Recently, Ian Balfour, a diamond historian, has speculated that this stone was fashioned from the so-called Hastings diamond,[17] a rough diamond weighing over one hundred carats that sparked a major political scandal in England during the reign of King George III. The stone was a gift to the king from one of the most influential and important Indian princes, the Nizam Ali Cawn. The scandal erupted when Warren Hastings, former Governor-general of India, was accused by his numerous enemies in Parliament of trying to bribe the king by securing the stone for him.

The King George IV diamond as mounted for the coronation crown of King George IV of England in 1821.

LAL QILA

A deep green round diamond of 72.76 carats was purchased by Harry Winston from an Indian dealer in 1949. Lal Qila, which means "Red Fort," was the greatest of all the Mogul imperial palaces. It was built in the seventeenth century by Shah Jahan, who was also responsible for the Taj Mahal, near the present site of Delhi, and served as the citadel for what was then Shah Jahan's new town of Shah Jahanabad. Unfortunately, nothing is known of the history of this rare colored diamond prior to its purchase by Mr. Winston. The stone was recut to 70.10 carats and given on memo to King Farouk of Egypt in 1951. After Farouk's overthrow in 1952, all legal efforts to retrieve the Lal Qila failed. There is no public record of its whereabouts since then. Because of the delicate nature of the legal proceedings, the story of the stone has never before been published.

LESOTHO

The Lesotho diamond was discovered by independent miner Ernestine Ramaboa in May 1967 at the Letseng-la-Terai diggings in Lesotho, southern Africa. The brownish rough weighed 601 carats and was sold at auction in Maseru, the capital of Lesotho, to a South African dealer who, in turn, sold it to a European dealer. The diamond was later purchased in Geneva by Harry Winston, who had it cut into eighteen stones, totaling 242.50 carats, in 1969; the largest three were a 71.73-carat emerald cut, a 60.67-carat emerald cut, and a 40.42-carat marquise. These three were sold individually as rings by 1970.

40.42 carats

60.67 carats

71.73 carats

LIBERATOR

This fine-quality, 155-carat rough diamond was discovered by three miners in the Gran Sabana diamond-bearing region of Venezuela in 1942. It was named in honor of Simón Bolívar, the nineteenth-century Venezuelan liberator.

Purchased in 1943 by Harry Winston, the rough diamond was cleaved into two pieces that were in turn fashioned into four stones: three emerald cuts, of 39.80 carats, 18.12 carats, and 8.93 carats, and a 1.44-carat marquise. Mr. Winston used the three smaller stones in an elaborate clip, and sold the largest stone mounted as a ring to Mrs. May Bonfils Stanton, daughter of the publisher and co-founder of the *Denver Post*, in 1946. In 1962, he reacquired this stone from Mrs. Stanton's estate and had the D-color diamond recut to a flawless 38.88 carats. The stone was purchased by an American client in 1966, who sold it at auction in New York City on December 7, 1972.

LOUIS XIV

This pear-shaped diamond reportedly belonged to Louis XIV of France. Although nothing of its history before Mr. Winston acquired it can be verified, it is probable that this was one of the Indian diamonds brought to Europe by the famous seventeenth-century gem merchant, Jean-Baptiste Tavernier.

In 1958, Harry Winston purchased the diamond from the estate of Thelma C. Foy, daughter of the founder of Chrysler Motor Corporation, and had it recut from its former 62.00 carats to a D-flawless 58.60 carats. (At the same time that he purchased the diamond, he also obtained from the Foy estate the 151-carat Burmese sapphire that is illustrated on page 189.) In 1959, the diamond was mounted as the center stone in a magnificent tiara that also contained six pear-shaped diamonds totaling 22 carats and 233 smaller diamonds totaling 120 carats. The Louis XIV diamond was exhibited at the Louvre in 1962 as part of the Ten Centuries of French Jewelry exhibition. In 1963, it was removed from the tiara and sold together with the 61.80-carat Winston diamond to Mrs. Eleanor Loder of Canada, who used the two stones in a pair of earrings. The Louis XIV diamond was sold in Geneva in 1981 from Mrs. Loder's estate.

MABEL BOLL

This emerald-cut diamond originally weighed 46.57 carats. It was once the property of Mabel Boll, a much-married American whose name was often in the news in the 1920s. In 1921, she was hailed by newspapers as "Broadway's most beautiful blonde." Mabel Boll collected sobriquets like she collected diamonds. In 1922, only four days after her marriage to Hernando Rocha, the Colombian coffee king, he presented her with a million dollars' worth of jewelry, mostly diamonds. The press then referred to her as the "$250,000-a-day bride." She earned her most lasting sobriquet, "Queen of Diamonds," because she frequently appeared in public wearing all of her jewels. It was said that the rings she wore on her left hand alone were worth more than $400,000.

After her death in 1949, Mr. Winston purchased the large emerald-cut diamond; according to Mabel Boll, the stone had originally been bought from Tiffany & Co. This unusually long stone (1⅜ inches by ⅝ inches) was recut to 45.67 carats, set in a ring, and then widely exhibited throughout the United States in Mr. Winston's Court of Jewels.

The diamond was sold in 1954 to a New York client. At the client's death in 1965, Mr. Winston reacquired the stone and had it recut to a flawless 44.76 carats. In 1966, the stone was sold to a European client. At that time, it was designed to be worn as a ring or as the center ornament to a bracelet containing an additional 112 emerald-cut diamonds weighing a total of 65.96 carats.

© DE BEERS CONSOLIDATED MINES

MCFARLIN

In 1954, from one of a number of rough diamonds that Harry Winston had purchased, he cut a greenish yellow 49.40-carat emerald-cut diamond. Unfortunately, company records do not indicate the weight of the particular piece of rough from which this single stone was fashioned. Mounted as the pendant to a necklace, surrounded by thirty one-carat round emeralds and some smaller diamonds, it was sold in 1956 to the McFarlin family of San Antonio, Texas. Upon the death of Mrs. McFarlin in 1961, the family donated the diamond to the Witte Memorial Museum in San Antonio. It was stolen from the museum in 1968 and never recovered.

NASSAK

As first known in India, the Nassak was a 90-carat triangular-shaped stone; at present it is a colorless 43.38-carat emerald cut. This world-renowned diamond was once among the treasures of a Hindu temple near the city of Nassak, where it is said to have been the eye of an idol of the Goddess Shiva, deity of both destruction and regeneration. After the Maharatta War of 1818, the diamond fell into the hands of the Duke of Hastings and became part of the booty taken from India. Christened the Nassak, the great diamond was sent to England. In 1831, during a period of severe economic depression, it was purchased by crown jewelers Rundell, Bridge & Company at auction. They had the stone recut to 80.59 carats for greater brilliance. In 1837, it again went to the auction block and was sold to the Duke of Westminster (at the same time he purchased the Arcots and the King George IV), who mounted it in the hilt of his dress sword. The stone remained in the Westminster family for almost a century, until it was sold to a Parisian jeweler. The jeweler brought the Nassak to America in 1926 for display. The diamond was later returned to Paris, where it was purchased by Harry Winston in 1940. Mr. Winston had the diamond recut to its present, flawless, 43.38-carat emerald-cut shape, and sold it to a New York jewelry firm in 1942.

In 1944, the Nassak was purchased by Mrs. William B. Leeds of New York City, who wore it in a ring. It was sold at auction in New York City in 1970.

NAPOLEON NECKLACE

The forty-seven diamonds in this famous necklace weigh a total of 275 carats. Napoleon I presented it to his wife, Empress Marie-Louise, a Hapsburg princess, on the birth of their son in March of 1811. With the death of Marie-Louise in 1847, the necklace passed to the Archduchess Sophie of Austria. She, in turn, left it to her third son, Archduke Karl Ludwig of Austria, upon her death in 1872. A French collector purchased the necklace from the grandson of Archduke Karl Ludwig, Prince Franz Joseph II of Liechtenstein, in 1948. Harry Winston acquired the piece in 1960 and sold it to Mrs. Marjorie Merriweather Post two years later. In accordance with Mrs. Post's instructions, the necklace was given to the Smithsonian Institution at her death in 1973.

© HAROLD & ERICA VAN PELT

NEPAL

Little is known about the beautiful 79.41-carat pear-shaped Nepal diamond. It is thought to have been mined in India's Golconda region and was in the possession of Maharaja Bir Shumsher Jung Bahadur Rana of Nepal in the late nineteenth century; it remained in the hands of Nepalese royalty until recent years. Unlike many of the rare treasures of Golconda, this gem did not leave the Indian subcontinent until this century.

Harry Winston purchased the diamond from an Indian dealer in 1957, at which time he had it recut slightly from its original 79.50-carat weight. Mounted in an elaborate pendant/brooch combination, the Nepal diamond was pictured in the April 1958 issue of *National Geographic*. In 1959, it was displayed at London's "Ageless Diamond" exhibition. That same year, the stone was sold to a European client as a pendant to a V-shaped diamond necklace that also contained 145 round diamonds weighing a total of 71.44 carats.

NIARCHOS

Originally called the Ice Queen, a 427-carat diamond of exceptionally fine color was found in the Premier Mine, South Africa, in 1954. In 1956, this piece of rough was sold to Harry Winston as part of an $8,400,000 parcel. The largest stone cut from this piece is a 128.25-carat D-flawless pear-shaped diamond with fifty-eight facets on the crown and pavilion and eighty-five additional facets around the girdle. That same year, this large stone was purchased by Stavros S. Niarchos, Greek shipbuilder and industrialist, whose name it currently bears. A 27.62-carat marquise and a 40-carat emerald cut were also obtained from the same rough and subsequently purchased by Mr. Niarchos.

COURTESY DE BEERS CONSOLIDATED MINES

NUR-UL-AIN TIARA

Several important pieces of jewelry were created by Harry Winston on the occasion of the marriage of his late Imperial Majesty Muhammad Reza Pahlavi Aryamihr Shahanshah and the Shanbanou Farah of Iran in 1958. When discussing any of the former Iranian Crown Jewels, superlatives become meaningless. It must be said, however, that the Nur-Ul-Ain tiara ranks among the most important pieces ever created. The name Nur-Ul-Ain means "Light of the Eye," and refers to the central diamond of the tiara, a stone of approximately 60 carats that is the largest oval rose-pink diamond on record. It undoubtedly came from the Golconda mines of southern India.

The recorded history of this stone begins in 1642 when Jean-Baptiste Tavernier, the French adventurer and gem merchant, reported seeing a large, approximately 300-carat, pink diamond for sale in southwest India. He referred to the stone as the "Great Table." The location of the Great Table was unknown until recently, when gemological investigation identified it among the Iranian Crown Jewels, now called the Darya-I-Nur, or "Sea of Light."

The Darya-I-Nur probably came into the possession of the Mogul emperors of India shortly after Tavernier saw it in 1642. In 1739, Nadir Shah of Persia invaded India and pillaged Delhi, its capital, for some fifty-eight days. The treasures of over a thousand years of Indian history, including the Darya-I-Nur, were

VAROUJ YAZEJIAN, PHOTO VAHE, TEHERAN

then carried off to Persia, the present-day Iran. By 1834, the Darya-I-Nur had been cut into two stones. The largest one, which retained the name Darya-I-Nur, is a crudely fashioned table-cut pink diamond of approximately 176 carats, and was one of the most celebrated stones in the Iranian Crown Jewels. The smaller oval stone was called the Nur-Ul-Ain.[18]

In 1958, Harry Winston was asked to create a tiara with the Nur-Ul-Ain as the center ornament. He had the Nur-Ul-Ain mounted in platinum surrounded by yellow, pink, blue, and colorless diamonds, above a border of undulating baguettes. Among the many treasures in this tiara are a 10-carat yellow pear-shaped diamond, directly above the Nur-Ul-Ain, and a cushion-cut pink diamond of approximately 19 carats, on the right top of the tiara.

OPPENHEIMER

COURTESY OF THE SMITHSONIAN INSTITUTION

This large pale yellow diamond crystal of 253.70 carats was found in 1964 at the Dutoitspan mine near Kimberley, South Africa. Such a well-formed crystal structure (octahedral) is rarely seen in a stone this size. The crystal has only a few black inclusions and is transparent.

Harry Winston purchased the crystal in 1964 and donated it to the Smithsonian Institution in memory of Sir Ernest Oppenheimer, chairman of the board of De Beers Consolidated Mines Ltd. from 1929 until 1957. The gift was, in Mr. Winston's words, "in tribute to a man who was my friend, who did inestimable service for me and other diamond dealers throughout the world and for millions of diamond owners as well."

POHL

Two major diamonds were found at the Elandsfontein diggings near Pretoria, South Africa, in January 1934: the 726-carat diamond called the Jonker and a 287-carat alluvial diamond known as the Pohl. According to the archives of the Kimberley Mine Museum, J. D. Pohl was the digger who found the diamond in the opposite side of the Little River from where the Jonker was found.

Harry Winston purchased this 287-carat rough diamond (at the same time he purchased the Jonker) and had it cut into several stones. The largest, called the Pohl, was a D-flawless emerald cut that weighed 38.10 carats. It was sold in 1943 to Bernice Chrysler Garbish, daughter of the founder of Chrysler Motor Corporation. It reappeared in October 1976, when it was auctioned in New York City on behalf of the estate of Bernice Garbish.

PORTUGUESE

Although this 127.01-carat emerald-cut diamond was believed to have belonged to the Portuguese royal family, no information has been uncovered to substantiate that story. We do know that on March 13, 1928, New York City newspapers reported the sale of a 127-carat emerald-cut diamond to the much-married Peggy Hopkins Joyce, who collected both wealthy husbands and large jewels. The stone was said to have come from the Kimberley mines of South Africa in 1912. The diamond was originally a cushion shape of approximately 150 carats when it first arrived in New York. Although the current form is described as an emerald cut, it is actually more of an octagon shape. Because its strong fluorescence gives the stone a soft blue tint, the diamond was advertised as the "largest blue diamond in the world" (*Vogue*, February 1924). The newspaper reports mentioned above state that when the diamond first came to the United States in 1912, there was much attendant publicity. However, a review of major newspapers for the period 1911–1913 failed to uncover any story related to the stone. Perhaps the diamond did have some connection with the royal family, which was not made public at the time.

Harry Winston purchased the diamond from Peggy Hopkins Joyce in 1951. The stone was displayed often at charitable functions throughout the United States in Mr. Winston's Court of Jewels. An international industrialist purchased the Portuguese diamond in 1957, then traded it back in 1962. In 1963, the Smithsonian Institution acquired the stone from Mr. Winston and placed it on permanent display.

FRED WARD—BLACK STAR

PORTER RHODES

Considered to be the finest African diamond found up to 1880, this 154-carat stone came from the claim of Mr. Porter Rhodes at the Kimberley Mine. In 1881, Mr. Rhodes visited Osborne House in London and showed it to Queen Victoria, who commented on its great purity and beauty. Empress Eugénie of France, who also saw the great diamond during this visit, remarked that it was "simply perfection," not knowing what to compare it with. At that time, it was generally believed that South African diamonds were inferior. The Empress Eugénie asked, "Are you sure the diamond is from South Africa, and have you not had it polished a little? I have always been under the impression that diamonds from the Cape were very yellow and worth but little."[19]

In 1926, the gem—by this time a 73-carat old-mine cut—was presented as a wedding gift by the Duke of Westminster to his third wife. Two years later it came into the possession of a London jewelry firm who had it refashioned in Amsterdam to a 56.60-carat emerald cut. It was sold to the Maharaja of Indore in 1937.

Harry Winston purchased the Porter Rhodes diamond in 1946 from the maharaja and subsequently sold it to a client in the United States. Mr. Winston repurchased the stone in 1957, and sold it to a client from Texas in 1958.

QAMAR-I-SALTANA

In 1970, Harry Winston fashioned two stones from a 108-carat rough diamond found in Sierra Leone. The larger stone, a D-flawless marquise, weighed 44.10 carats. It was called the Qamar-I-Saltana, a Persian title meaning "moon of the kingdom" that is given only to women of the highest rank. The diamond was set as a ring (as illustrated on pages 41 and 115) and sold in 1971. The smaller stone, a D-flawless pear shape that weighed 6.35 carats, was also sold in 1971.

QUEEN OF GOLCONDA

Harry Winston purchased this 49.62-carat D-flawless marquise diamond in 1960. It had belonged to the maharajas of Boroda for many generations: they had received it originally as a special token from the mines of Golconda. The stone eventually came into the possession of a French noble family, who sold it to a French gem collector after World War II.

Mr. Winston sold the diamond in 1963 but repurchased it in 1974. It was sold again that same year.

ROVENSKY

In one of the most spectacular jewelry sales of the century, the estate of Mrs. Mae C. Rovensky, wife of the industrialist and banker John E. Rovensky, was auctioned in New York in January of 1957. Mrs. Rovensky, whose beauty was similar to that of the famous nineteenth-century British actress Lily Langtry, was married four times. She is notorious for the unusual trade she made in 1916, when she was married to wealthy industrialist Commodore Morton F. Plant. She gave the deed to her mansion on Fifth Avenue and Fifty-Second Street to Cartier in exchange for two strands of oriental pearls, 55 and 73 pearls respectively, then valued at one and a half million dollars.

From Mrs. Rovensky's estate, Harry Winston purchased a 31.40-carat D-color antique cushion-cut diamond. It was recut slightly to 31.20 carats and then sold to Mrs. Marjorie Merriweather Post that same year. The stone was auctioned in New York on April 20, 1982, as the Merriweather Post diamond.

SHAH OF PERSIA

The recorded history of this 99.52-carat cushion-shaped yellow diamond dates back to 1650 in India. It was said to have been part of Nadir Shah's plunder after his sack of Delhi in 1739 (see "Nur-Ul-Ain Tiara"). Shortly after World War I, the stone was brought to America by General V. Starosselky, a Russian military expert who had been loaned to Persia by Czar Nicholas II. The diamond was reportedly presented to General Starosselky by the Ahmad Shah for his excellent command of the Persian army. The stone was subsequently purchased by an American family, who held it in a bank vault for thirty years. In 1957, Harry Winston purchased the stone from a Los Angeles dealer; at the time it was mounted in an antique combination pendant/brooch. Mr. Winston sold the diamond to a client from the Middle East in 1965.

SHAKESPEARE MARQUISE

In 1969, Mr. Winston purchased a rough diamond weighing 154 carats. In 1970, two diamonds were cut from the rough: a 50.62-carat D-flawless marquise, named in honor of William Shakespeare, and a 7.11-carat D-flawless marquise. Later that year, Mr. Winston sold the Shakespeare Marquise set in a ring with two shield-shaped diamonds on either side of the stone; he repurchased the stone in 1978 and sold it again that same year.

STAR OF THE EAST

Interestingly, there are at least three different accounts of the early history of this 94.80-carat D-color pear shape, none of which can be fully verified. Some gem historians feel that the stone was one of a number of large diamonds discovered in South Africa at the end of the last century that were probably cut in Amsterdam and were subsequently sold to Louis Cartier. A second account starts in the mid-seventeenth century, when French gem merchant Tavernier purchased a 157-carat rough diamond known as the Ahmedabad. After Tavernier reportedly disposed of the stone in Persia, it disappeared. Again, there are two versions of the history of the stone from this point on. The first theory is that a stone cut from the Ahmedabad rough appeared in the possession of Sultan Abdul Hamid II of the Ottoman Empire (now Turkey), who wore it in his turban. During the period of unrest that preceded the Young Turks' rebellion in 1909, the Star of the East, together with the Hope and the Idol's Eye, appeared in Paris for sale. Duped by the agent to whom he had entrusted the stones for safe passage, the sultan reportedly lost all three stones as well as the money they brought.

However, in October of 1908, there appeared in a German newspaper (*Die Woche*) a photograph of a fabulous diamond necklace owned by the Gaekwar (a term analogous to Maharaja) of Baroda. The caption calls the diamond the Star of the East, which adds confusion to an already questionable history. The Gaekwar of Baroda owned both the English Dresden (a 76-carat pear shape) and the Star of the South (a 129-carat oval), yet the shape of the stone pictured in *Die Woche* is quite like that of the Star of the East.

The Star of the East is shown here set in a necklace with two emerald pendants. The large diamonds (28 carats each) in the accompanying earrings can replace the emerald drops. The ring shown here is the 44.10-carat Qamar-I-Saltana diamond.

In this 1881 photo, the Gaekwar of Baroda is shown wearing a magnificent diamond necklace. The largest stone strongly resembles the Star of the East and was so identified in 1908 by the German newspaper Die Woche.

Photographs as early as 1881 show the Gaekwar wearing these fabulous stones. In any event, one can only speculate as to how long the Barodas owned the Star of the East, if this was indeed the stone illustrated.

In late 1908, a young American couple were enjoying an extended honeymoon in Paris. They had each received $100,000 from their fathers as a wedding gift. The bridegroom was Edward (Ned) B. McLean, son of a multi-millionaire publisher; the bride was Evalyn Walsh, the daughter of a miner who, in her own words, "struck it rich."[20] Evalyn Walsh McLean loved fine jewels, while her husband had little interest in them. When Pierre Cartier went to their hotel suite to show them the 94.80-carat Star of the East, the new Mrs. McLean was captivated. "Ned," she said, in mock despair, "it's got me. I'll never get away from the spell of this." "A shock might

break the spell," said Ned. "Suppose you ask the price of this magnificence."[21] But Evalyn Walsh McLean refused to hear the objection in her husband's voice, and proceeded to purchase the Star of the East, using all of her "pin money" and some of his: the price was $120,000. In later years, she often wore it on the same necklace with the Hope diamond, which she had acquired in 1911. Photographs from the second and third decades of this century (see, for example, the illustration on page 74) show her wearing the Star of the East in an incredible "aigrette" (a jeweled headpiece popular in the late nineteenth and early twentieth centuries) with what appears to be a Bird of Paradise feather in a diamond bandeau.

Harry Winston purchased the Star of the East from Mrs. McLean's estate in 1949. In 1951, Mr. and Mrs. Winston were on the Riviera with King Farouk of Egypt and his new queen, Narriman, and invited them for dinner to their home on a promontory overlooking the Mediterranean. As Mr. Winston told the story:

> "It was all a great success and, as things do on such occasions, proceedings continued well into the wee small hours. Sometime about four in the morning, the early dawn was coming and Farouk and I walked out on the terrace. The morning star was there in the east—in glowing brilliance. At the time, I happened to have a magnificent diamond 'The Star of the East' at ninety-four carats. I loved it dearly. I told Farouk about it. And one thing led to another—the stars in the sky, the star in the east, my 'Star of the East,' and the stars in Narriman's eyes—and Farouk said that he would like to buy the diamond. We settled on $1,125,000.00."[22]

The stone was given on memo to the king, but at the time of his overthrow in 1952, it still had not been paid for (see page 32 for further details). It took Mr. Winston many years of investigation and litigation to reclaim the diamond.

Harry Winston sold the Star of the East in 1969. In 1977, the owner asked Mr. Winston to remount the diamond so that it could be worn as a pendant to a V-shaped diamond necklace. The diamond came back into the possession of Harry Winston, Inc., in 1984.

STAR OF SIERRA LEONE

At 970 carats, this is the third largest rough diamond, and the largest alluvial diamond, ever discovered. It was found on February 14, 1972, at the separator plant of the Diminco Mine at Yengema, Sierra Leone. Harry Winston purchased the Star of Sierra Leone in 1972. He had it cut into seventeen diamonds with a total weight of 238.48 carats; thirteen of the stones were flawless. Originally, the largest stone was a 143.20-carat emerald cut, of fine color but flawed. Mr. Winston felt that such a large stone should be flawless, and after several weeks of careful deliberation he ordered it recut. The top was sawed horizontally to remove the imperfections. The bottom piece was refashioned to a D-flawless emerald cut of 35.52 carats. From the top piece that had been removed, six diamonds were fashioned; five of these were D-flawless. These six stones—weighing a total of 21 carats—were used in the Star of Sierra Leone brooch, arranged like the petals of a flower. The brooch was sold in Europe in 1975.

Ultimately, the largest stone recovered from the Star of Sierra Leone rough was a flawless pear shape of 53.96 carats. It was sold in 1975 as the pendant to a V-shaped necklace that also contained ninety-eight brilliants weighing a total of 41 carats.

STAR OF INDEPENDENCE

In 1975, Harry Winston purchased an extraordinary piece of South African rough weighing 204 carats. After rolling the rough diamond between his fingers for a few minutes, Mr. Winston quietly announced that it would produce a large, perfect faceted stone. Indeed, the rough was cut into a 75.52-carat D-flawless, pear-shaped diamond in the spring of 1976. In honor of the American Bicentennial, Ronald Winston christened the stone the Star of Independence.

Within weeks after the faceting was completed, the stone was sold for four million dollars—making it the most expensive diamond sold up to that time. It was set as a pendant to a V-shaped necklace with thirty-eight pear-shaped diamonds totaling 29 carats and thirty-five round diamonds totaling 32 carats.

STAR OF THE SOUTH

This 14.37-carat D-color diamond, a kite-shaped table cut, is an example of a rarely seen ancient Indian style of polishing diamonds in which both the top and bottom are bounded by broad parallel facets.

The diamond was sold to Evalyn Walsh McLean in 1928. She was, as she said at the time, "feeling blue from all the trouble of making million-dollar ends meet."[23] Buying a new piece of jewelry always cheered her up. She was told when she purchased the diamond that the stone had most recently belonged to another well-known American family, who had said that it was always called the Star of the South (not to be confused with the 129-carat diamond owned by the Baroda family and also referred to as the Star of the South). The diamond was set as the center ornament of a ruby-and-diamond bracelet, with sixteen emerald-cut diamonds weighing a total of 26 carats and sixteen emerald-cut rubies weighing 35 carats total.

Harry Winston purchased the bracelet from the estate of Mrs. McLean in 1949. The rubies and diamonds were removed, and used in another bracelet. The Star of the South was recut from its original 15.28 carats and sold as the center ornament to a multi-strand pearl bracelet in 1950. Mr. Winston repurchased the bracelet in May of 1978 from the estate of Mrs. George F. Baker. The diamond was mounted as a ring and sold in 1981.

STAR OF SULEIMAN

In 1957, Harry Winston purchased a 149-carat rough diamond at the request of a Saudi Arabian client. A 93.86-carat oval diamond was cut from the rough stone and named for the great caliph of Baghdad, Suleiman the Magnificent. Mounted as a pin, the Star of Suleiman was sold that same year.

STONEWINS

In response to a special order from a Saudi Arabian client, Harry Winston purchased a 232-carat piece of rough in 1957. Two emerald-cut diamonds, weighing 86.40 carats and 78.54 carats, respectively, were the result. Mr. Winston christened the diamonds the Stonewins after his country estate. The 78.54-carat stone was set as a pendant with a star-burst motif of baguettes and round diamonds. The 86.40-carat stone was set as a pendant to a V-shaped diamond necklace.

TAYLOR-BURTON

This 69.42-carat pear-shaped D-flawless diamond was cut by Harry Winston from a 241-carat piece of rough found in 1966 at the Premier Mine in South Africa. Mrs. Paul Annenberg Ames purchased the stone from Mr. Winston in 1967. In 1969, the stone was sold at auction in New York. It was resold the following day to Richard Burton for his wife, Elizabeth Taylor. The diamond was subsequently named the Taylor-Burton. It has since been resold.

TITAN OVAL

In September of 1978, Harry Winston purchased a rough South African diamond weighing 98 carats. From it was fashioned a 51.31-carat E-flawless oval diamond, which was finished in January of 1979, shortly after Mr. Winston's death. It was mounted as a ring and sold in October of 1979.

VARGAS

It is a grand and magnificent coincidence of nature that the sixth and seventh largest rough diamonds ever discovered (the 726.60-carat Vargas and the 726-carat Jonker) weighed almost the same—only six-tenths of a carat separated them. The Vargas was discovered in 1938 in the San Antonio River, municipality of Coromandel, Minas Gerais, Brazil, by a native prospector and his partner, a farmer. It was named in honor of the then-president of Brazil, Getulio Vargas (1930–1945, 1951–1954). Harry Winston caught a plane to Brazil only a matter of hours after reading a small newspaper item reporting the discovery of the diamond. No sooner had he landed in Rio de Janeiro than he was on a ship to Antwerp, as the dealer to whom the stone was originally shown had just shipped it there. Having secured passage on a faster ship, Mr. Winston arrived in Antwerp before the diamond. As a result, he was able to examine and buy the rough stone before it was officially offered to any other dealer. In 1941, he had it cut into twenty-nine stones. All the important ones were emerald cuts.

The largest stone fashioned from this piece of rough weighed 48.26 carats, and is now known as the Vargas diamond. It was sold to Mrs. Robert Windfohr of Ft. Worth, Texas, in 1944. The diamond was repurchased by Harry Winston in 1958 and recut to a flawless 44.17 carats. It was sold again in 1961.

Seven of the other emerald-cut diamonds—ranging from 18 to 31 carats (a total of 176 carats)—were used in a diamond bracelet created in 1947 for an Indian maharaja.

The Vargas diamond necklace, with seven emerald-cut diamonds totaling 176 carats that were all faceted from the same piece of rough.

In 1952, the maharaja asked Mr. Winston to remount these seven stones in a unique diamond necklace. Two additional emerald-cut diamonds, weighing 23 carats (sold in 1946) and 19 carats (sold in 1944), were set as rings.

"An amusing thing happened here when we split the Vargas," Winston relates. "My chief cleaver was nervous about breaking up the $700,000 diamond, so I didn't dare tell him in advance when we were going to cut. Then one day I suggested casually that he practice a bit with the steel rod that we use to strike the cleaving wedge. After about twenty minutes, he said the stroke felt just right, so I told him to go ahead."

Mr. Winston couldn't tell who was sweating harder, the cleaver or himself.

"Just as he brought the rod down to strike, it was as though an invisible hand stopped his arm, for the tap he gave the Vargas wouldn't have dented a cream puff. He was the color of the stone itself, and I yelled, 'Hit it. Hit it.' So he upped again with the rod and came down with the neatest blow I ever saw. The diamond couldn't have fallen apart better, and neither could that cleaver. He took one look at the job and passed out cold."[24]

WASHINGTON

In 1976, Harry Winston had two D-color pear-shaped diamonds fashioned from a 342-carat piece of South African rough. One stone weighed 89.23 carats and was set as a pendant to a diamond necklace. This stone was christened the Washington diamond in honor of the first American president. The second stone, a flawless 42.98 carats, was set in a ring. Both diamonds were sold in 1977.

WINSTON

A 155-carat colorless rough diamond was found in the Jagersfontein Mine, South Africa, in 1952. The following year, Harry Winston purchased the rough in London. It was subsequently cut to a D-flawless 62.05-carat pear shape and sold in 1959 to the King of Saudi Arabia, who returned it the next year. Mr. Winston had it recut to 61.80 carats and matched it with the 58.60-carat Louis XIV diamond. The two were sold as a pair of earrings to Mrs. Eleanor Loder of Canada in 1963. In November 1981, they were auctioned in Geneva, Switzerland, with a final price of $7,300,000.

Mr. Winston enjoyed relating the following story about his experience with the Winston diamond:

> "One of my clients was the late King of Saudi Arabia. He had a large court, four wives, and something like eighty concubines. At one time I had a 62-carat diamond that I loved very much—it was a pear shape. The Saudi Arabian king was an extremely valuable client. To satisfy his large court, his dealings with us ran into millions. In the normal course of business with this regal figure, I told him about the extraordinarily valuable and beautiful diamond. The king said that he would like to have it and a deal was concluded. The gem was specially wrapped and handed over to the king.
>
> "A year and a half later the king arrived in Boston for a special eye treatment at the clinic there, and I was summoned to see him. At that time, I sold two million dollars' worth of jewelry to him. Just before I left, he handed me a wrapped parcel. It was vaguely familiar. When I looked at it I realized that it hadn't been opened for one and a half years.
>
> " 'Mr. W,' said the king, 'I hope you will credit me with this against the jewels I've bought from you.' I turned to the king and said: 'Why

return this to me? It's the most beautiful diamond.' The king replied: 'Well, you see, just as you want to live, so I want to live. I have four wives, and if I give one stone to one wife, well, my life won't be worth a moment's peace—unless of course you have three others like this.' Mr. Winston shook his head and dutifully took back the stone.

"Three weeks later, in the normal course of business, I was asked to value some jewelry from the estate of the late Thelma C. Foy, who was a daughter of Jack Chrysler, the motorcar tycoon. I opened up the case, and to my amazement, I saw what happened to be an exact duplicate of my Winston diamond. It was a perfect match. The strangest thing was that whereas my diamond was 62 carats, this was 60 carats. The difference was so infinitesimal.

"They made a perfect match, so I had them made up as a pair of earrings. In due course, a Canadian client of mine heard that I had something special. When she saw the earrings she burst out 'These are mine. There can't be any doubt about it.' She told her husband, and the deal was closed immediately."[25]

WINSTON HEART SHAPE

In 1969, Harry Winston fashioned a 59.25-carat emerald cut and five smaller diamonds from a piece of rough that weighed 206 carats. The large emerald cut was sold in 1970 and repurchased by Harry Winston, Inc., in 1980. At that time, to improve the quality of the diamond, the firm had the stone recut to a unique heart shape of 40.97 carats. It was sold that same year to a client in Europe.

AN EMPIRE BUILT ON JEWELRY

"But most things aren't as beautiful as jewels. Nothing gives a woman so much beauty. Their value in money is something you never think of. They mean so much more. Partly it is an association with the person who gave them to you—but not all. They come to have their own meaning."

PEGGY GUGGENHEIM[1]

Like his predecessors Peter Carl Fabergé and Louis Cartier, Harry Winston set his own standards of originality in fine jewelry. All three men, each in his own way, helped elevate the jeweler's art to new heights of grandeur through bold, innovative designs and superior workmanship.

Mr. Winston's creativity sprang from a desire to display the finest-quality gemstones in the most elegant settings possible. While he admired the interesting jewelry designs of the Art Deco style that predominated in the 1920s, Mr. Winston wanted his settings to place more emphasis on the beauty of the gemstones themselves. For the most part, the Art Deco pieces were made by taking flat, solid pieces of metal and sawing out holes for the gems. Even though a craftsman might put hours of painstaking labor into the piece, the finished product had little flexibility and no sense of dimension. The jewelry that followed Art Deco did feature larger stones, but lacked detail and, Winston felt, distinction. Sometimes called "retro-modern,"[2] this jewelry was characterized by plain, heavy settings mounted with large stones.

Mr. Winston was dissatisfied with these heavy settings, and longed for a better fabrication method, one that could give his jewelry more life. His inspiration for a new method of designing and constructing jewelry came during one Christmas season near the end of World War II. Arriving home one evening, he suddenly took notice of a holly wreath that was hanging from his front door. He saw how the holly leaves themselves shaped the wreath, and wondered what would happen if the *gemstones*, rather than the metal, shaped the piece of jewelry. Winston immediately set his designers to work to develop new, softer designs. For these new designs, he gradually developed a fabrication device that would become his hallmark in the jewelry industry: fine, hand-made, flexible wire settings of platinum or gold. These independent prong settings enabled distinctive arrangements of variously shaped diamonds and colored stones, giving a new freedom to the art of jewelry fabrication and helping to establish an entirely new trend in jewelry design. It was as if the gemstones could now be woven into the precious metal that held them.

The subtle grace of the handmade settings gave Mr. Winston's jewelry a delicacy that further enhanced the gemstones they contained. In addition, the new wire settings could be used to create three-dimensional pieces with some of the world's most dazzling gems sparkling at every angle. One client was so thrilled with a ruby and diamond necklace and bracelet that she had purchased that she ordered the same design in sapphire and diamond. Mr. Winston was particularly proud that these settings gave him the flexibility to create "bracelets which can be crumpled like a sweater and not one stone will touch the other."[3]

For his jewelry, Mr. Winston assembled collections of rare gemstones that would have intimidated most others in the field. He would sometimes wait years to obtain just the right stones to complete a particular piece. Harry Winston often surrounded these large diamonds or colored stones with a frame of smaller diamonds: He felt that just as a painting by a famous master deserved a beautiful frame, so did one of his precious stones. This "frame" has become another characteristic of the Winston style.

The photographs and drawings of Harry Winston jewelry that follow are testimony to his innovative genius in jewelry design. Fewer than ten percent of these photos have ever been published before. This dazzling display represents but a glimpse of the magnificent jewelry that has been the trademark of the house of Winston for over fifty years.

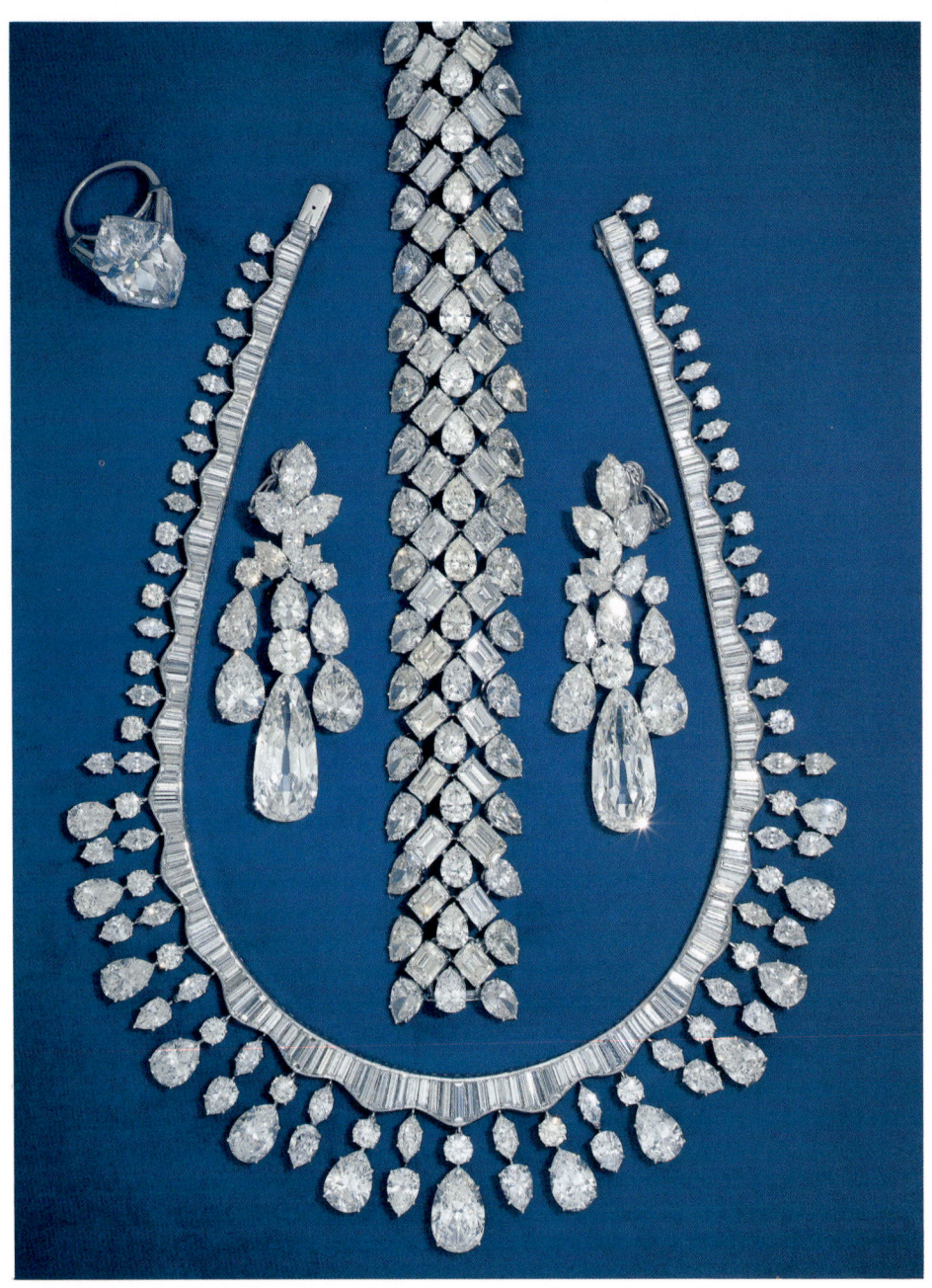

Diamond Bracelet
1959
85 Diamonds
 120 carats

Diamond Necklace
1958
307 Diamonds
 90 carats

Diamond Earrings
1961
28 Diamonds
 80 carats
2 Largest Diamonds
 31.42 carats

Diamond Ring
1960
1 Diamond
 25.36 carats

Sapphire and Diamond Necklace
1982
20 Sapphires
 210 carats
405 Diamonds
 129 carats

PINK AND SALMON
CONCH PEARL AND DIAMOND NECKLACE
1985
Pear-shaped Pink Conch Pearl
Round Salmon Conch Pearl
White Cultured Pearls
222 Diamonds, 13 carats

PINK AND SALMON
CONCH PEARL AND DIAMOND EARRINGS
1985
Tops, One Pink and One Salmon Conch Pearl
Drops, One Pink and One Salmon Conch Pearl
190 Diamonds, 13 carats

SAPPHIRE AND DIAMOND EARRINGS
1971

26 Sapphires, 76 carats
2 Largest Sapphires, 36.57 carats
26 Diamonds, 25 carats

SAPPHIRE AND DIAMOND COLLAR
1979

53 Sapphires, 187 carats
Largest Sapphire, 21.04 carats
126 Diamonds, 162 carats

Emerald and Diamond
Necklace
1959
Emerald-cut Emerald
 20.61 carats
Hexagon Emerald
 22.25 carats
15 Emeralds
 95 carats
404 Diamonds
 117 carats
Pear-shaped Emerald
 15.97 carats

Diamond Necklace
1979
231 Diamonds
 141 carats

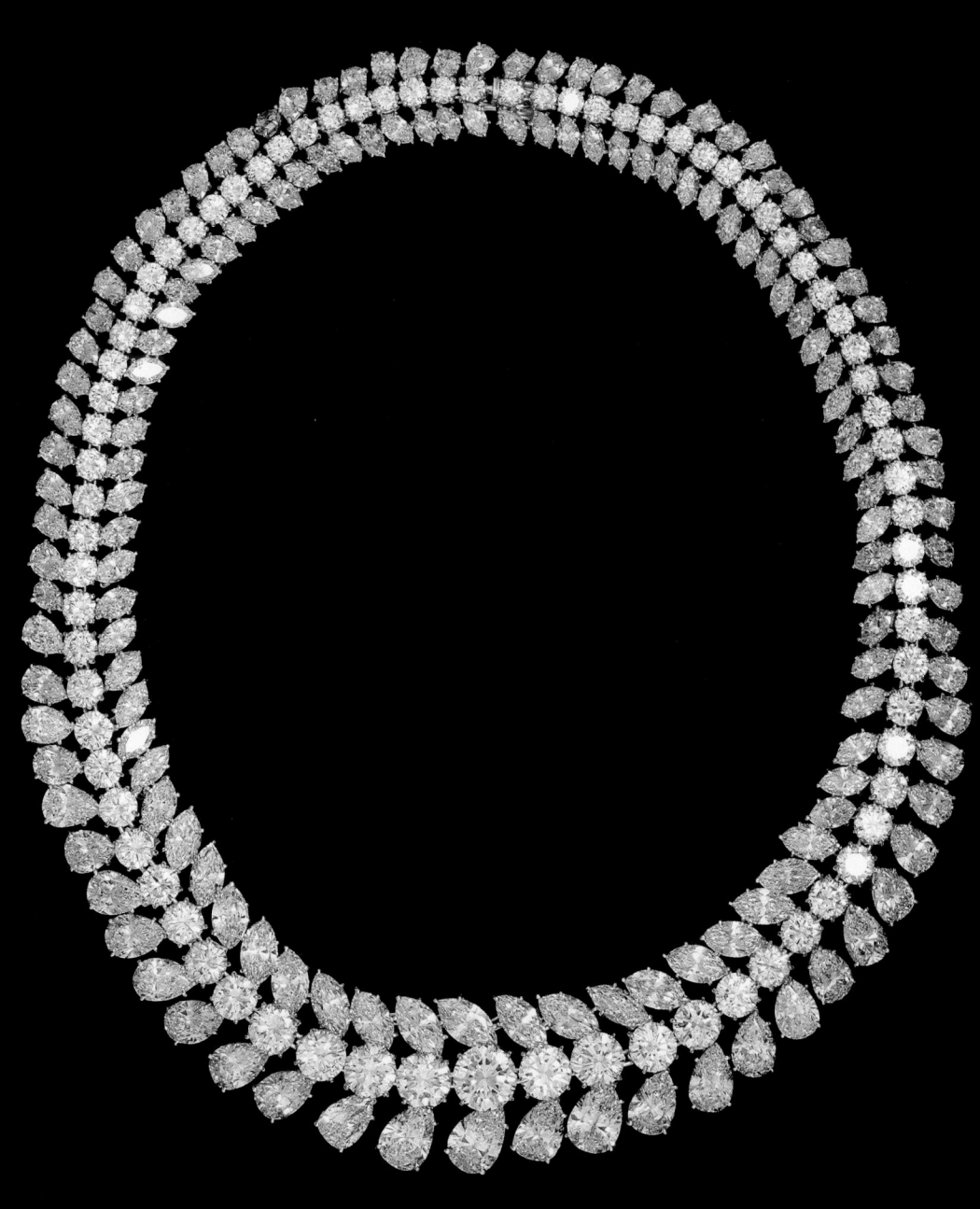

YELLOW DIAMOND EARRINGS
1976

2 Canary Diamonds, 48.50 carats
64 White Diamonds, 22 carats

GRAY PEARL AND DIAMOND NECKLACE
1981

40 Gray Tahitian Cultured Pearls, 10-14 mm
574 Diamonds, 68 carats

GRAY PEARL AND DIAMOND EARRINGS
1981

2 Gray Tahitian Cultured Pearls, 12 mm
56 Diamonds, 6 carats

SOUTH SEA CULTURED PEARL
AND DIAMOND NECKLACE
1984

98 South Sea Cultured Pearls, 11–16 mm
12 Diamonds, 8 carats

SOUTH SEA CULTURED PEARL
AND DIAMOND EARRINGS
1984

2 South Sea Cultured Pearls, 15 mm
26 Diamonds, 9 carats

SOUTH SEA CULTURED PEARL
AND DIAMOND RING
1984

South Sea Cultured Pearl, 15 mm
14 Diamonds, 6 carats

Ruby and Diamond
Necklace
1985

28 Heart-shaped Rubies
  70 carats
17 Heart-shaped Diamonds
  30 carats
126 Diamonds
  57 carats

Diamond Bracelet
1974

14 Diamonds
  98 carats
Largest Diamond
  14.64 carats

Diamond Necklace-Bracelet
Combination
1966

140 Diamonds
  112 carats

Blue Sapphire Ring >
1984
Blue Sapphire, 35.26 carats

Ruby Ring
1980
Ruby, 18.42 carats

Yellow Diamond Ring
1984
Canary Diamond, 29.16 carats

Padparadscha Sapphire Ring
1983
Padparadscha Sapphire, 32.50 carats

Yellow and
White Diamond Bracelet
1984
7 Canary Diamonds, 20 carats
119 White Diamonds, 23 carats

Ruby and Diamond Bracelet
1976
48 Rubies, 73 carats
96 Diamonds, 52 carats

Emerald and Diamond Bracelet
1967
11 Emeralds, 41 carats
11 Diamonds, 31 carats

COURTESY OF SOTHEBY-PARKE-BERNET, INC.

< Diamond Necklace
1964
393 Diamonds, 126 carats

Emerald, Cultured Pearl,
and Diamond Necklace
1985

Emerald, 12 carats
10 Black Cultured Pearls, 9–13 mm
10 White Cultured Pearls, 9–13 mm
230 Diamonds, 23 carats

Emerald, Cultured Pearl,
and Diamond Earrings
1985

2 Emeralds, 0.80 carat
2 Black Cultured Pearls, 11 and 16 mm
2 White Cultured Pearls, 11 and 16 mm
118 Diamonds, 15 carats

Ruby and Diamond Necklace
1985

42 Rubies, 40 carats
114 Diamonds, 50 carats

Ruby and Diamond Earrings
1985

14 Rubies, 9 carats
28 Diamonds, 9 carats

DIAMOND AND ONYX NECKLACE
1985
9 Canary Diamonds, 79 carats
18 Onyx
711 Diamonds, 27 carats

DIAMOND AND ONYX EARRINGS
1985
2 Canary Diamonds, 5 carats
4 Onyx
64 Diamonds, 5 carats

DIAMOND AND ONYX RING
1985
Canary Diamond, 9 carats
2 Onyx
72 Diamonds, 2 carats

RUBY AND DIAMOND BRACELET
1961
81 Rubies, 67 carats
36 Diamonds, 28 carats

RUBY AND DIAMOND NECKLACE
1962
205 Rubies, 73 carats
198 Diamonds, 36 carats

EMERALD AND DIAMOND EARRINGS
1963
2 Emeralds, 44 carats
58 Diamonds, 16 carats

Diamond Necklace
1980

283 Diamonds
164 carats

Diamond Necklace
1985

191 Diamonds
53 carats

Diamond Earrings
1984

74 Diamonds
18 carats

DIAMOND NECKLACE
1978

234 Diamonds
112 carats

EMERALD AND DIAMOND NECKLACE
1979

33 Emeralds, 94 carats
Largest Emerald, 18.65 carats
319 Diamonds, 105 carats

EMERALD AND DIAMOND BRACELET
1980

9 Emeralds, 31 carats
81 Diamonds, 22 carats

EMERALD AND DIAMOND EARRINGS
1980

2 Emeralds, 4 carats
30 Diamonds, 9 carats

RUBY AND DIAMOND BRACELET
1967

34 Rubies
35 carats
158 Diamonds
28 carats

Diamond Necklace
1959
274 Diamonds
110 carats

Diamond Necklace
1959
218 Diamonds
136 carats
Largest Pear Shape
10 carats

SAPPHIRE AND DIAMOND NECKLACE
1978

9 Sapphires
  116 carats
256 Diamonds
  112 carats

SAPPHIRE AND DIAMOND BRACELET
1978

8 Sapphires
  53 carats
152 Diamonds
  55 carats

YELLOW DIAMOND BRACELET
1984

7 Canary Diamonds
  20 carats
119 Colorless Diamonds
  23 carats

EMERALD AND DIAMOND BRACELET
1973

14 Emeralds
  15 carats
56 Diamonds
  33 carats

COURTESY OF THE ROYAL ONTARIO MUSEUM, TORONTO, CANADA—
LEIGH WARREN, PHOTOGRAPHER

Ruby and Diamond Necklace
1981

15 Rubies
  60 carats
Largest Ruby
  13.29 carats
166 Diamonds
  56 carats

Ruby and Diamond Earrings
1981

2 Rubies
  13 carats
44 Diamonds
  17 carats

Emerald and Diamond Tiara, 1958. *Created for the marriage of his late Imperial Majesty Muhammed Reza Pahlavi Aryamihr Shahanshah and the Shanbanou Farah of Iran.*

Diamond Earrings
1973

26 Diamonds
  28 carats

Emerald and Diamond
Necklace
1958

12 Emeralds
 57 carats
425 Diamonds
 110 carats

Diamond Bracelet
1971

266 Diamonds
 152 carats

Diamond Earrings
1972

84 Diamonds
 88 carats

Diamond Bracelet
1965
80 Diamonds
68 carats

Diamond Necklace with
Emerald and Diamond Pendant
1969
Emerald, 68.90 carats
272 Diamonds, 119 carats

Ruby and Diamond Necklace
1956
84 Rubies
70 carats
247 Diamonds
45 carats

Ruby and Diamond Necklace
1983

Largest Ruby, 14 carats
24 Rubies, 42 carats
232 Diamonds, 46 carats

Ruby and Diamond Earrings
1985

4 Rubies, 8 carats
70 Diamonds, 9 carats

Diamond Necklace
1959

567 Diamonds
106 carats

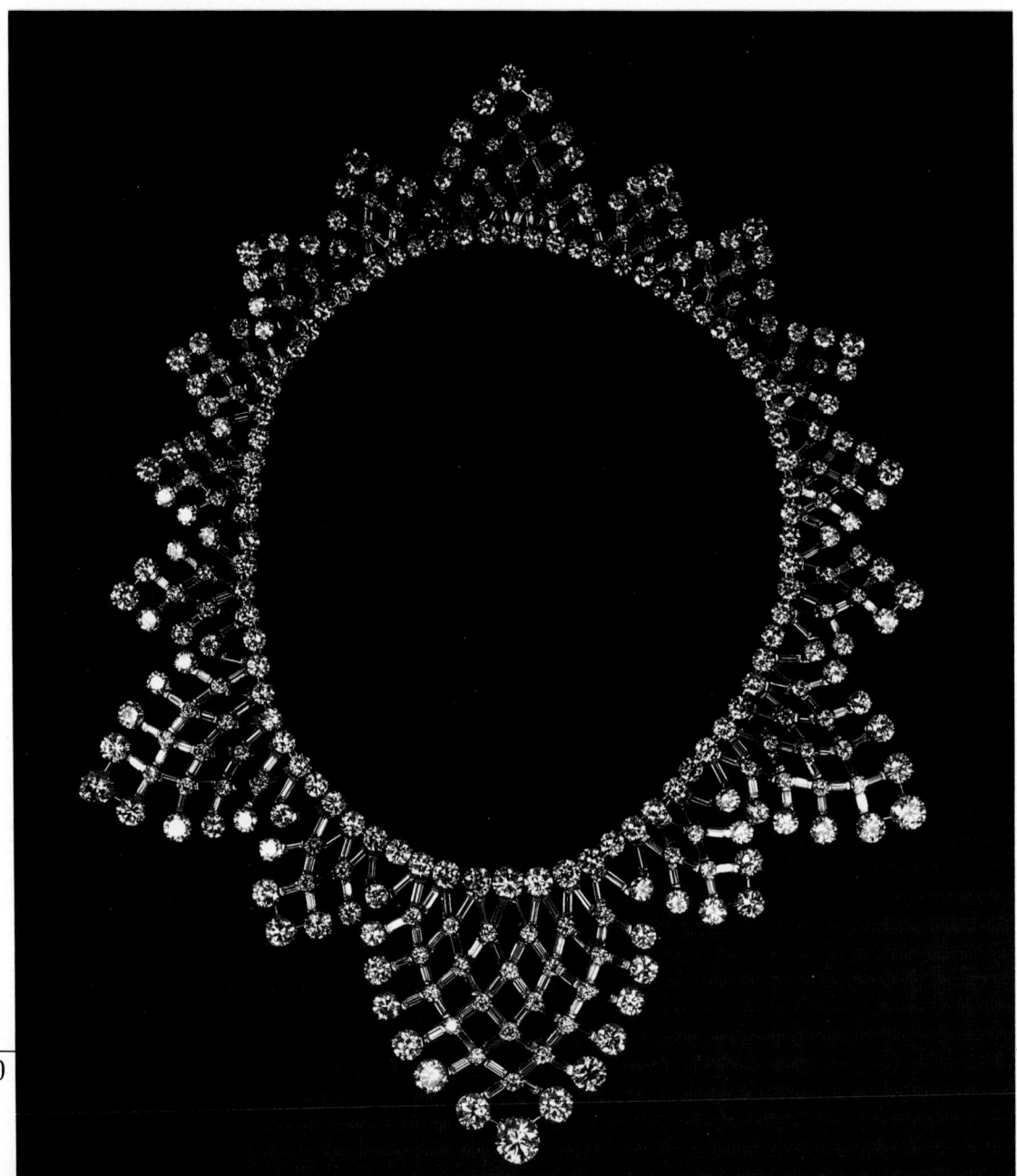

EMERALD, YELLOW SAPPHIRE,
AND DIAMOND RING
1985

Cabochon Emerald, 7 carats
2 Yellow Sapphires, 2 carats
28 Diamonds, 9 carats

EMERALD, YELLOW SAPPHIRE,
AND DIAMOND NECKLACE
1985

12 Cabochon Emeralds, 38 carats
10 Yellow Sapphires, 19 carats
266 Diamonds, 56 carats

RUBY AND DIAMOND NECKLACE
1981

16 Burma Rubies, 111 carats
Largest Ruby, 17.02 carats
255 Diamonds, 173 carats

RUBY AND DIAMOND EARRINGS
1981

2 Burma Rubies, 4 carats
40 Diamonds, 16 carats

© HAROLD & ERICA VAN

RUBY AND DIAMOND BRACELET
1978

12 Rubies
 55 carats
12 Diamonds
 19 carats

DIAMOND BRACELET
1959

260 Diamonds
 58 carats

DIAMOND NECKLACE
1961

128 Diamonds
 168 carats

DIAMOND BRACELET
1961

78 Diamonds
 70 carats

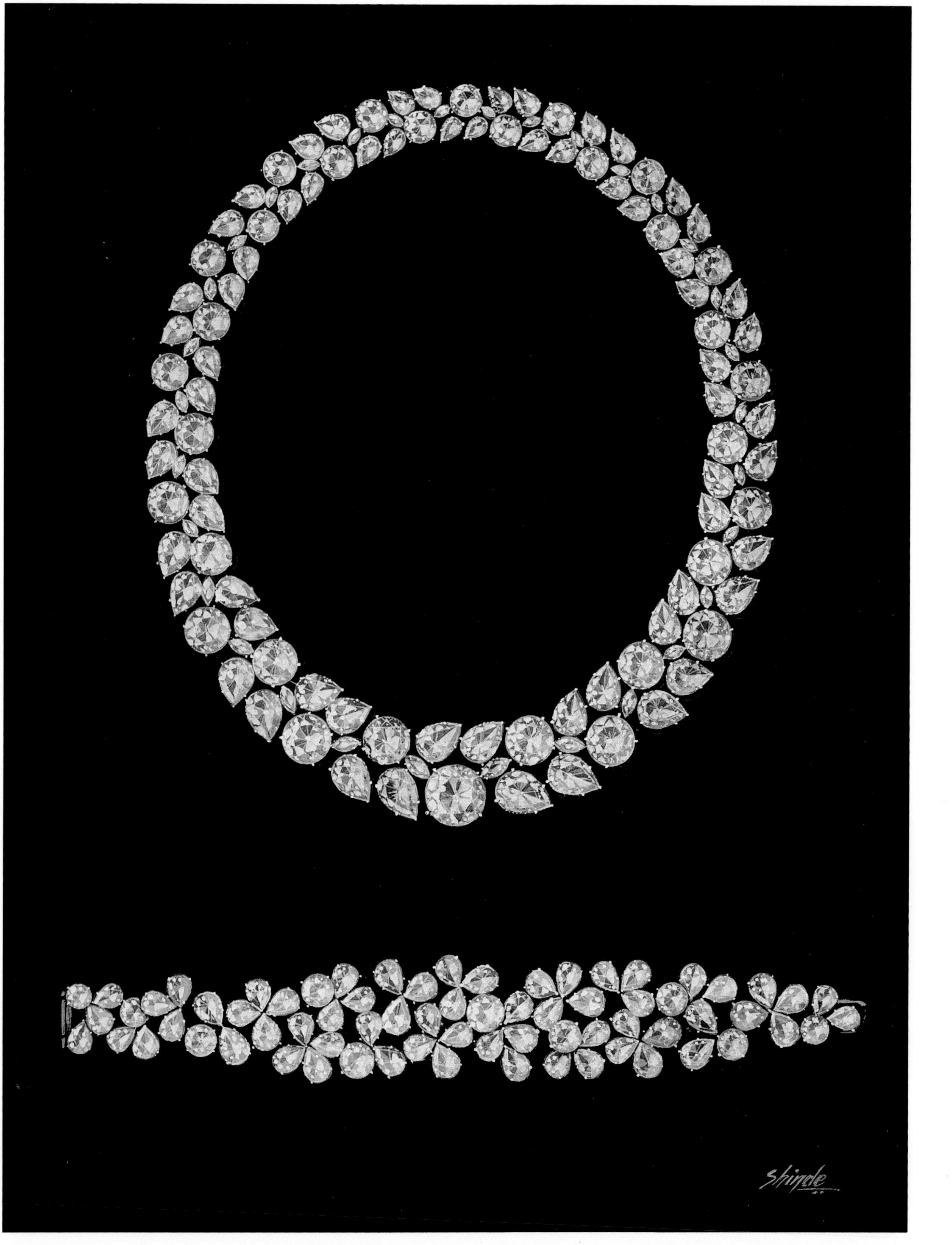

◁ **Diamond Necklace**
1973

252 Diamonds
　284 carats
Largest Diamond
　20.72 carats

Emerald and Diamond ▷
Necklace
1979

14 Emeralds
　56 carats
Largest Emerald
　12.88 carats
424 Diamonds
　172 carats

⟨ EMERALD AND DIAMOND
EARRINGS
1970

2 Emeralds
　73 carats
2 Emeralds
　8 carats
348 Diamonds
　36 carats

RUBY AND DIAMOND ⟩
NECKLACE
1979

8 Rubies
　66 carats
323 Diamonds
　96 carats

SAPPHIRE AND DIAMOND
BRACELET
1959

9 Sapphires
　53 carats
45 Diamonds
　20 carats

⟨ Sapphire and Diamond
  Bracelet
  1968

  5 Sapphires
    77 carats
  172 Diamonds
    60 carats

  Diamond Necklace ⟩
  1957

  147 Diamonds
    146 carats

⟨ Ruby and Diamond Bracelet
  1976

  48 Rubies
    73 carats
  96 Diamonds
    52 carats

DIAMOND
NECKLACE-BRACELET
COMBINATION
1961
207 Diamonds
57 carats

BLUE AND WHITE
DIAMOND CLIP
1947

Blue Diamond
23.23 carats
White Diamond
23.91 carats
69 White Diamonds
14 carats

BLUE AND WHITE
DIAMOND CUFFLINKS
1947

Blue Triangular Diamond
11.04 carats
White Triangular
Diamond
10.23 carats
Blue Pear-shaped
Diamond
8.15 carats
White Pear-shaped
Diamond
8.01 carats

Emerald and Diamond Necklace >
1978

32 Emeralds, 58 carats
32 Diamonds, 23 carats

Diamond Earrings
1970

2 Emerald-cut Diamonds
    65 carats
2 Pear-shaped Diamonds
    20 carats
2 Diamonds
    2 carats

Diamond Necklace
1978

316 Diamonds
    56 carats

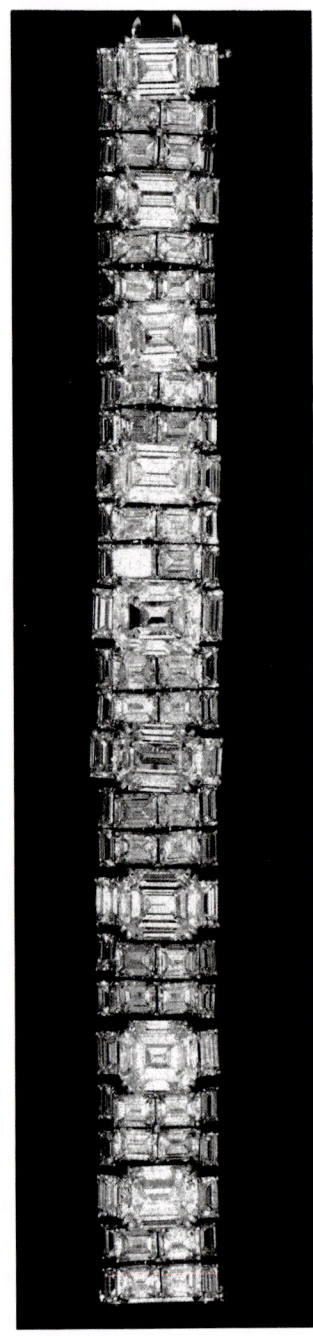

SAPPHIRE AND DIAMOND NECKLACE
1979
40 Sapphires, 94 carats
272 Diamonds, 62 carats

SAPPHIRE AND DIAMOND EARRINGS
1979
10 Sapphires
  25 carats
64 Diamonds
  17 carats

DIAMOND BRACELET
1975
99 Diamonds
  141 carats

DIAMOND BRACELET
1953
286 Diamonds
  86 carats

Diamond Necklace with Sapphire Pendant

Sapphire Pendant
1960
Sapphire, 151.03 carats
91 Diamonds, 20 carats

Diamond Necklace
1957
537 Diamonds, 64 carats

Diamond Necklace
1979
355 Diamonds
98 carats

Sapphire and Diamond Bracelet
1980
6 Sapphires
85 carats
114 Diamonds
36 carats

EMERALD AND DIAMOND NECKLACE
1967

22 Emeralds, 91 carats
28 Diamonds, 52 carats

EMERALD AND DIAMOND PENDANT
1984

Emerald, 37 carats
20 Diamonds, 15 carats

EMERALD AND DIAMOND EARRINGS
1977

2 Emerald Drops, 49 carats
2 Emerald Tops, 11 carats
68 Diamonds, 16 carats

EMERALD AND DIAMOND BRACELET
1967

11 Emeralds, 41 carats
11 Diamonds, 31 carats

RUBY AND DIAMOND EARRINGS
1977

32 Rubies
   41 carats
62 Diamonds
   33 carats

EMERALD AND DIAMOND NECKLACE
1978

86 Emeralds, 55 carats
168 Diamonds, 75 carats

EMERALD AND DIAMOND BRACELET
1978

40 Emeralds, 23 carats
80 Diamonds, 43 carats

EMERALD AND DIAMOND EARRINGS
1978

8 Emeralds, 14 carats
26 Diamonds, 17 carats

RUBY AND DIAMOND TIARA
(converts to necklace)
1962

149 Rubies
   123 carats
307 Diamonds
   75 carats

⟨ Diamond Bracelet
1957
24 Diamonds
 90 carats

Sapphire and Diamond ⟩
Necklace
1964
54 Sapphires
 76 carats
112 Diamonds
 67 carats

Sapphire and Diamond
Earrings
1964
6 Sapphires
 13 carats
8 Diamonds
 13 carats

⟨ Emerald and Diamond
Bracelet
1967
144 Emeralds
 64 carats
66 Diamonds
 69 carats

DIAMOND BRACELET
1959

102 Diamonds
64 carats

RUBY AND DIAMOND NECKLACE
1965

178 Rubies, 153 carats
91 Diamonds, 64 carats

COURTESY OF CHRISTIE'S

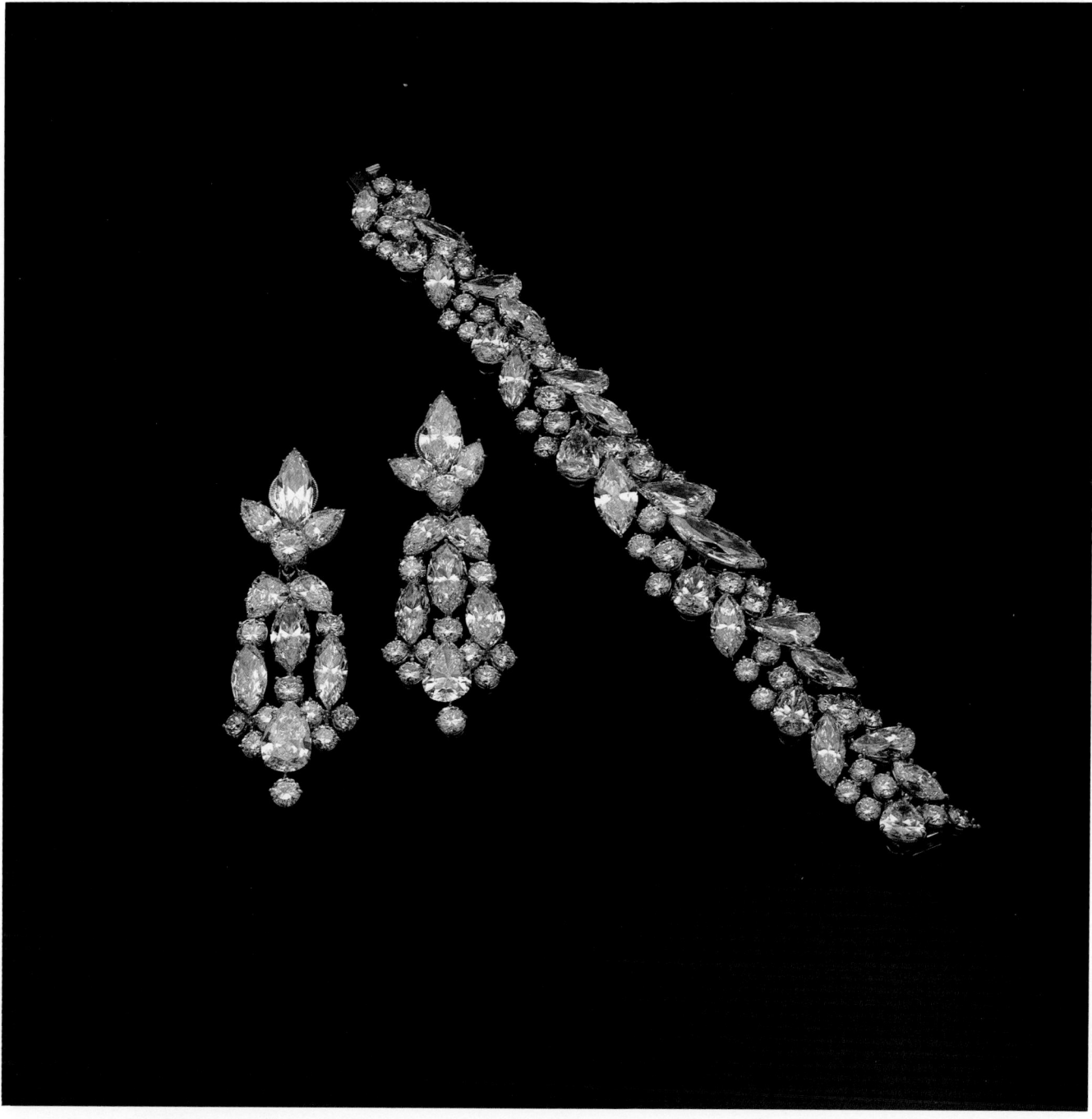

DIAMOND BRACELET
1980

72 Diamonds
    67 carats

DIAMOND EARRINGS
1980

40 Diamonds
    42 carats

Emerald and Diamond
Necklace
1956

142 Emeralds
59 carats
Largest Emerald
18.95 carats
157 Diamonds
36 carats

Diamond Dog Collar
1976
159 Diamonds, 238 carats

Sapphire and
Diamond Earrings
1977

2 Sapphires
113 carats
44 Diamonds
17 carats

Ruby and Diamond Necklace
and Earrings
1978

Necklace
50 Rubies
  124 carats
Largest Ruby
  16.87 carats
310 Diamonds
  66 carats

Earrings
18 Rubies
  50 carats
2 Largest Rubies
  23.07 carats
176 Diamonds
  27 carats

Ruby and Diamond Earrings
1969

176 Rubies
  52 carats
80 Diamonds
  14 carats

Diamond Bracelet
1976

70 Diamonds
  128 carats

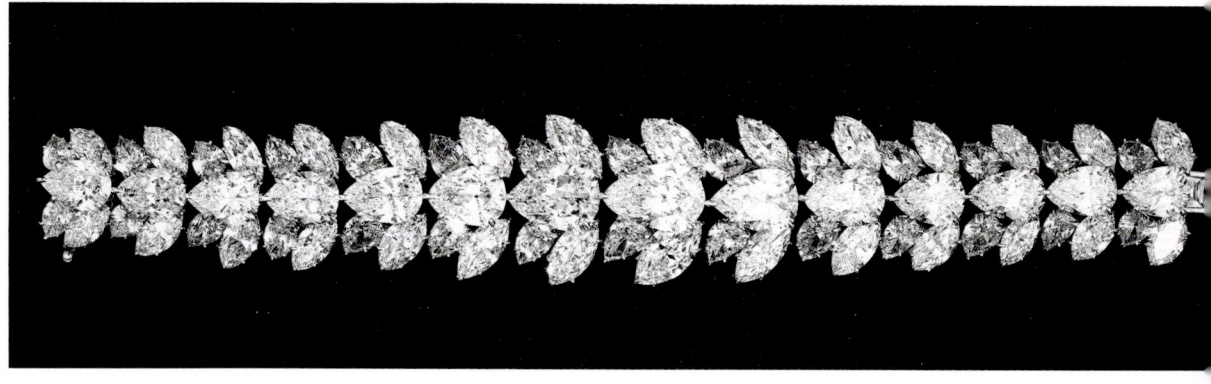

200

DIAMOND BRACELET
1971

150 Diamonds, 73 carats
7 Emerald-cut Diamonds, 97 carats

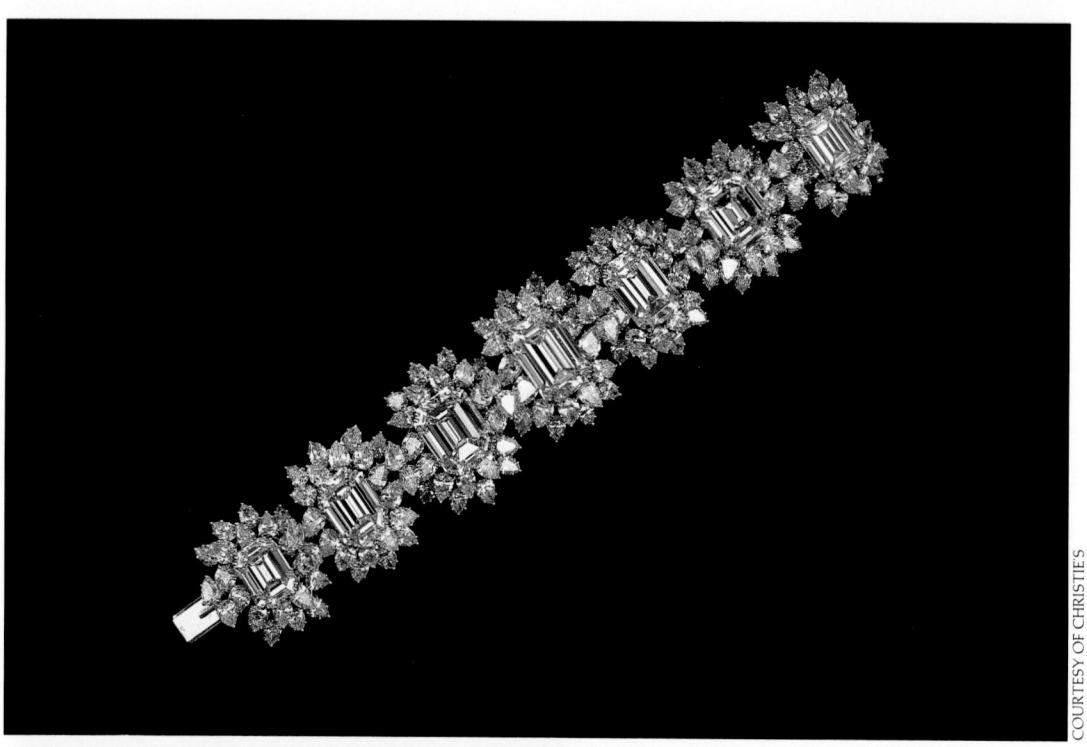

COURTESY OF CHRISTIE'S

**BRIOLETTE EMERALD
AND DIAMOND EARRINGS**
1957

2 Hexagon Briolette Emeralds
  7.43 carats
2 Briolette Emerald Drops
  26 carats
32 Diamonds
  14 carats

BLUE AND WHITE DIAMOND NECKLACE
1964

Blue Diamond, 51.84 carats
116 White Diamonds, 120 carats

BLUE AND WHITE DIAMOND BRACELET
1964

Blue Diamond, 45.85 carats
91 White Diamonds, 87 carats

BLUE AND WHITE DIAMOND EARRINGS
1964

2 Blue Diamonds, 23.29 carats
26 White Diamonds, 28 carats

EMERALD AND DIAMOND
NECKLACE
1975

5 Emeralds
  93 carats
453 Diamonds
  150 carats

EMERALD AND DIAMOND
NECKLACE
1977

7 Emeralds
  48 carats
Largest Emerald
  24.61 carats
231 Diamonds
  90 carats

SAPPHIRE AND DIAMOND
NECKLACE
1980

95 Sapphires
  79 carats
572 Diamonds
  103 carats

SAPPHIRE AND DIAMOND
BRACELET
1980

29 Sapphires
  17 carats
140 Diamonds
  17 carats

SAPPHIRE AND DIAMOND
EARRINGS
1980

24 Sapphires
  18 carats
170 Diamonds
  19 carats

DIAMOND NECKLACE
1979

202 Diamonds
  181 carats
Largest Diamond
  20.48 carats

SAPPHIRE AND DIAMOND EARRINGS
1971

2 Pear-shaped Sapphires, 36 carats
14 Sapphires, 21 carats
26 Diamonds, 28 carats

Clockwise, starting top left:

DIAMOND EARRINGS
1983

26 Diamonds
 15 carats

DIAMOND EARRINGS
1983

38 Diamonds
 26 carats

DIAMOND EARRINGS
1983

14 Diamonds
 14 carats

DIAMOND EARRINGS
1983

18 Diamonds
 16 carats

DIAMOND EARRINGS
1979

12 Diamonds
 11 carats

DIAMOND NECKLACE
1962

39 Round Brilliants
 44 carats
280 Baguettes
 60 carats

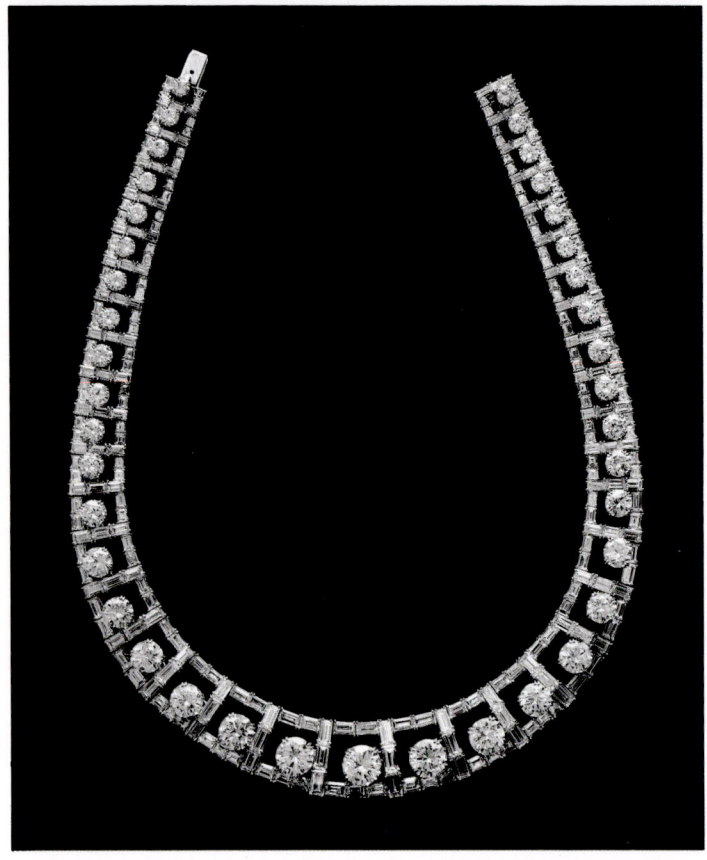

DIAMOND NECKLACE
1973

6 Pear-shaped Diamonds
  43 carats
275 Diamonds
  174 carats

Miss Merrill
EMERALD AND DIAMOND NECKLACE
1980

34 Emeralds, 97 carats
644 Diamonds, 128 carats

EMERALD AND DIAMOND EARRINGS
1978
2 Pear-shaped Emeralds, 22 carats
54 Diamonds, 38 carats

Miss Rumbough
EMERALD AND DIAMOND NECKLACE
1981

26 Emeralds, 19 carats
212 Diamonds, 33 carats

EMERALD AND DIAMOND EARRINGS
1978

18 Emeralds, 7 carats
28 Diamonds, 11 carats

DIAMOND BRACELET
1970

126 Diamonds
  102 carats

PHOTOGRAPHY BY VICTOR SKREBNESKI.   COURTESY TOWN AND COUNTRY MAGAZINE.

American actress and socialite Dina Merrill and her daughter Nina Rumbough wearing emerald and diamond jewelry supplied by Harry Winston, Inc.

APPENDIX

NOTES

INTRODUCTION

1. Joan Y. Dickinson, *The Book of Diamonds* (New York: Crown Publishers, 1965), p. vii.

NO STONE UNTURNED

1. Copyright 1949, Consolidated Music, renewed 1976.
2. Lillian Ross, "The Big Stone: A Profile of Harry Winston," *The New Yorker,* May 8, 1954, p. 43.
3. From the title "King of Diamonds," by Elsie and Harmon Tupper, *Cosmopolitan,* April 1947, p. 48.
4. James Stewart-Gordon, "Harry Winston: Ace of Diamonds," *Reader's Digest,* January 1978, p. 188.
5. Tupper, "King of Diamonds," p. 109.
6. Ibid.
7. Dickinson, *Book of Diamonds,* p. vii.
8. Ibid.
9. Tupper, "King of Diamonds," p. 112.
10. Ibid.
11. Ross, "The Big Stone," May 15, 1954, pp. 61–62.
12. Ross, "The Big Stone," May 8, 1954, p. 67.
13. Herbert Brean, "Golconda on E. 51 Street," *Life,* March 17, 1952, p. 67.
14. Ross, "The Big Stone," May 15, 1954, p. 43.
15. Madeleine Van Biljon, "Setting Pretty," *Fair Lady,* July 12, 1967, p. 25.
16. Evalyn Walsh McLean, *Father Struck It Rich* (Boston: Little, Brown & Co., 1936), p. 155.
17. Tupper, "King of Diamonds," p. 110.
18. Stewart-Gordon, "Ace of Diamonds," p. 186.
19. Ross, "The Big Stone," May 8, 1954, p. 44.
20. Ross, "The Big Stone," May 15, 1954, pp. 53–54.

AN EMPIRE BUILT ON DIAMONDS

1. Ross, "The Big Stone," May 8, 1954, p. 52.
2. Lord Twining, *History of the Crown Jewels of Europe* (London: Batsford Press, Ltd., 1960), p. 161.

3. Jules Grad, "Baleful Hope Diamond Finds a New Owner," *New York Herald Tribune* (Paris), April 15, 1949, p. 5.
4. George C. Blakely, *The Diamond* (New York and London: Paddington Press Ltd., 1977), p. 29.
5. Ibid.
6. Susanne Steinem Patch, *Blue Mystery: The Story of the Hope Diamond* (Washington, D.C.: Smithsonian Institution Press, 1976).
7. *New York Times*, "Hope Diamond's Owner Lost," November 17, 1909, p. 1.
8. *New York Herald*, "Hope Diamond is Not Lost, He Says," November 18, 1909, p. 9.
9. *New York Times*, "Hope Diamond Goes Cheap," June 29, 1909, p. 1.
10. Evalyn Walsh McLean, *Father Struck It Rich* (Boston: Little, Brown, and Co., 1936), pp. 175, 178, and 295.
11. Ibid., p. 170.
12. Ibid., p. 301.
13. A. N. Wilson, "Prince of Diamonds, King of Raconteurs," *International Diamond Annual*, Vol. 1 (Johannesburg, South Africa: Diamond Annual Ltd. [Pty.], 1971), p. 177.
14. Elsie and Harmon Tupper, "King of Diamonds," pp. 48 and 50.
15. Lord Twining, *History of the Crown Jewels of Europe*, pp. 160–163.
16. Ibid., p. 160.
17. Ian Balfour, "The Hastings Diamond," *Indiaqua*, Vol. 34, No. 1, 1983, pp. 129–133.
18. V. B. Meen and A. D. Tushingham, *Crown Jewels of Iran* (Toronto: University of Toronto Press, 1968), pp. 26–29.
19. For the complete story of this encounter, see Edwin W. Streeter, *Great Diamonds of the World* (London: George Ben & Co., 1882), pp. 144–149.
20. McLean, from the title *Father Struck It Rich*.
21. McLean, *Father Struck It Rich*, p. 155.
22. Wilson, "Prince of Diamonds, King of Raconteurs," p. 179.
23. McLean, *Father Struck It Rich*, p. 295.
24. Tupper, "King of Diamonds," pp. 48–112.
25. Wilson, "Prince of Diamonds, King of Raconteurs," p. 180.

AN EMPIRE BUILT ON JEWELRY

1. Laura Riley, "America's Most Fabulous Jewels," *Ladies' Home Journal*, July 1958, p. 110.
2. Ettagale Lauré and Donald S. McNeil, comps., "Designing Your Design Vocabulary," *Jewelers' Circular-Keystone*, September 1983, p. 172.
3. Madeleine Van Biljon, "Setting Pretty," *Fair Lady*, July 12, 1967, p. 27.

BIBLIOGRAPHY

Abbott, Mary. *Jewels of Romance and Renown*. London: T. Werner Laurie, Ltd., 1933.

Balfour, Ian. "The Hastings Diamond." *Indiaqua*, Vol. 34, No. 1, 1983, pp. 129–133.

"Big Rocks." *Time*, April 18, 1949.

Birmingham, Stephen. *The Grand Dames*. New York: Simon & Schuster, 1982.

Blakely, George C. *The Diamond*. New York and London: Paddington Press Ltd., 1977.

Blakeslee, Howard W. "New Diamond History Nearing: Vargas Stone to Go on Block." *Birmingham (Alabama) News*, February 16, 1941.

Bracker, Milton. "The Hope Diamond is Off in the Mail." *New York Times*, November 9, 1958.

Bracker, Milton. "Winston Gives Hope Diamond to Smithsonian for Gem Hall." *New York Times*, November 8, 1958.

Brean, Herbert. "A Rich Display for Moving Day." *Life*, April 8, 1960, p. 50.

Brean, Herbert. "426 Carats of Icy Blue." *Life*, February 20, 1956, pp. 57–60.

Brean, Herbert. "Golconda on E. 51 Street." *Life*, March 17, 1952, pp. 67–82.

Bruton, Eric. *Diamonds*. Radnor, Pennsylvania: Chilton Press, 1970.

Burggraf, Helen. "Harry Winston Out to Restyle Its Image." *Crain's New York Business*, November 25, 1985, pp. 1 and 81.

"Buys $300,000 Gem." *New York Journal*, March 13, 1928.

"By Registered Mail: The Hope Diamond." *Life*, November 24, 1958, p. 53.

Cattelle, W.R. *The Diamond*. London: John Lane, 1911.

Cooper, Hal. "Diamond Tiara Often Worn by Royalty Brings Record $308,000." (Seattle, Washington) *Times*, June 25, 1959.

"Costly Luster—That $2,000,000 Diamond Deal." *The London Illustrated News*, March 9, 1957.

"Countess László Széchényi, 78, Former Gladys Vanderbilt, Dies." *New York Times*, January 30, 1965.

"Countess László Széchényi Left Bulk of Her Estate to Four Daughters." *New York Times*, February 14, 1965.

"Court of Jewels' Famed Gems Will Be Shown Here." *San Antonio (Texas) Evening News*, January 16, 1952.

Craft, Loren. "A $2 Million Teardrop." *New York Daily News*, March 17, 1957.

"Dealer in the Fabulous: Harry Winston." *New York Times*, November 8, 1958.

Dickinson, Joan Y. *The Book of Diamonds*. New York: Crown Publishers, 1965.

"Dies und Das." *Die Woche*, October 17, 1908.

Dieulefait, Louis. *Diamonds and Precious Stones*. Translated from the French by Fanchon Sanford. New York: Scribner, Armstrong & Co., 1874.

"$11,000,000 Gem Show Opens in San Antonio." *San Antonio (Texas) Evening News*, February 8, 1952.

"Elverson Gems Sold." *New York Times*, December 5, 1930.

Emanuel, Harry. *Diamonds and Precious Stones*. London: John C. Hotten, 1867.

"Famous Ruby Sold to Jeweler Here." *New York Times*, December 21, 1930.

Feuchtwanger, Lewis. *A Popular Treatise on Gems*. New York: D. Appleton & Co., 1859.

"First Cut in Vargas Diamond Is Successful, Expert Lost 6 Pounds Over $300,000 Piece." *New York Times*, May 16, 1941.

Gaal, Robert A.P. *The Diamond Dictionary*, 2nd Edition. Santa Monica, California: Gemological Institute of America, 1977.

Grad, Jules B. "Baleful Hope Diamond Finds a New Owner." *New York Herald Tribune*, Paris, April 15, 1949.

Graf, Richard. "Hope Diamond Still Cursed." *New York Journal American*, November 9, 1958.

Heiniger, Ernst and Jean. *The Great Book of Jewels*. New York: N.Y. Graphic Society, 1974.

Hertz, B. *A Catalogue of the Collection of Pearls and Precious Stones Formed by Henry Philip Hope Esq.* London: William Clowes & Sons, 1839.

"Hope Diamond Goes Cheap." *New York Times*, June 25, 1909.

"Hope Diamond Is Not Lost, He Says." *New York Herald*, November 18, 1909.

"Hope Diamond Not Lost." *New York Times*, November 20, 1909.

"Hope Diamond, Other Gems Sold to City Jeweler by McLean Estate." *New York Times*, April 16, 1949.

"Hope Diamond's Owner Lost." *New York Times*, November 17, 1909.

"Huge Diamond Becomes Family's Best Friend." *Ebony*, January 1969, pp. 112–115.

Jeffries, David. *A Treatise on Diamonds and Pearls*. London: 1751.

Joyaux Provenant de la Collection Habib. Collection catalogue published in Paris, June 1909.

Joyce, Peggy Hopkins. *Men, Marriage and Me*. New York: Macaulay Co., 1930.

Kellogg, Cynthia. "Record Foy Collection of Furnishings." *New York Times*, May 9, 1960.

"Killam Jewel Collection Bought by Harry Winston." *New York Herald Journal Tribune*, February 14, 1967.

Knox, Sanka. "5th Ave. Mansion Will Go on Sale." *New York Times*, December 14, 1956.

Knox, Sanka. "Necklace Is Sold on Bid of $385,000." *New York Times*, January 24, 1957.

"Largest Brazil Diamond Here." *New York Times*, July 9, 1940.

Lauré, Ettagale, and Donald S. McNeil, comps. "Designing Your Design Vocabulary." *Jewelers' Circular-Keystone*, September 1983, p. 172.

Legrand, Jacques. *Diamonds, Myth, Magic and Reality.* New York: Crown Publishers, 1980.

"Lucky Baldwin Ruby Sold to New Yorker." *New York Times*, December 7, 1930.

MacLaurin, Barbara. "Ronald Winston Wants the Lost Generation." *International Herald Tribune*, September 15, 1983, p. 32.

McGlashan, Ian. "The Story of the Hope Diamond." *Lapidary Journal*, January 1980, pp. 2242–2249.

McLean, Evalyn Walsh. *Father Struck It Rich.* Boston: Little, Brown & Co., 1936.

Mawe, John. *A Treatise on Diamonds and Precious Stones.* London, 1813.

Mawe, John. *A Treatise on Diamonds and Precious Stones*, 2nd Edition. London, 1823.

Meen, V.B., and A. D. Tushingham. *Crown Jewels of Iran.* Toronto, Canada: University of Toronto Press, 1968.

"Millions in Gems Sold." *New York Sun*, December 6, 1930.

"Miss Joyce Gets Big Gems." *New York Times*, March 13, 1928.

"Miss Miller Much Criticized." *New York Times*, March 18, 1928.

"Miss Vanderbilt Now a Countess." *New York Times*, January 26, 1908.

"Miss Vanderbilt's Wedding Gift Displayed Before Close Friends." *New York Herald*, January 25, 1908.

"Mrs. Byron C. Foy, a Society Leader." *New York Times*, August 21, 1957.

"Mrs. C. P. Huntington Weds in Family." *New York Times*, July 17, 1913.

"Mrs. Gary's Jewels Are Sold to Dealer." *New York Times*, December 10, 1936.

"Mrs. Huntington Had $1,274,904 in Jewels." *New York Times*, July 16, 1926.

"Mrs. J. E. Rovensky of Newport Dead." *New York Times*, July 22, 1956.

Murray, John. *A Memoir on the Diamond.* London: Relfe & Fletcher, 1839.

"Mystery Veils History of Mabel Boll, Diamond Queen and Air Adventuress." *New York World*, April 15, 1928.

Nadelhoffer, Hans. *Cartier: Jeweller Extraordinary.* New York: Abrams Press, 1984.

"Nancy Miller Weds Former Maharaja in Gorgeous Rites." *New York Times*, March 18, 1928.

"New Yorker Pays $700,000 for Lucky Baldwin Jewels." *The New York World*, December 6, 1930.

"Old M. F. Plant Home Leased to Jeweler." *New York Times*, October 4, 1911.

"$1,000,000 in Jewels and Afraid to Wear a Single Pearl." *New York Evening Journal*, March 26, 1927.

"$1,000,000 Was Cut to $150,000 Say Boll Heirs." *New York Daily News*, April 15, 1949.

Ostier, Marianne. *Jewels and the Woman*. New York: Horizon Press, 1958.

Parke-Bernet Galleries, Inc. *The Fabulous Collection of Precious-Stone Jewelry of the Late May Bonfils Stanton*. New York: Parke-Bernet Galleries, Inc., 1962.

Patch, Susanne Steinem. *Blue Mystery: The Story of the Hope Diamond*. Washington D.C.: Smithsonian Institution Press, 1976.

"Peggy Joyce Pays $300,000 For Necklace." *New York Daily News*, March 13, 1928.

Pignatelli, Prince. "When Mabel Boll and Peggy Joyce Meet—Oh? ?X!!X!." (New York) *American*, August 11, 1928.

Pollack, Isaac. *The World of the Diamond*. Hicksville, New York: Exposition Press, 1975.

"Puzzle of Hope Diamond." *New York Times*, November 18, 1909.

"Queen of Diamonds Arrives with Gems." *New York Times*, October 27, 1927.

"Queen of Diamonds Dies." *New York Times*, April 11, 1949.

Rice, Stanley. *The Life of Sayaji Rao III: Maharajah of Baroda*. London: Oxford University Press, 1931.

Riley, Laura. "America's Most Fabulous Jewels." *Ladies' Home Journal*, July 1958, pp. 43–114.

Ross, Lillian. "The Big Stone: A Profile of Harry Winston." *The New Yorker*, May 8, 1954, pp. 36–69.

Ross, Lillian. "The Big Stone: A Profile of Harry Winston." *The New Yorker*, May 15, 1954, pp. 45–73.

Runyon, Damon. "Harry Winston, Diamond Champ." (New York) *American*, April 24, 1936.

Sotheby & Co. *Catalogue of Highly Important Jewels*. London: Sotheby & Co., June 25, 1959.

Sotheby-Parke-Bernet, Inc. *The Magnificent Jewelry Collection of Mrs. Enid Haupt*. New York: Sotheby-Parke-Bernet, Inc., December 7, 1972.

Stanfill, Francesca. "Harry Winston: The Wizard of Rocks." *W Magazine*, January 24, 1975, pp. 4–5.

Stewart-Gordon, James. "Harry Winston: Ace of Diamonds." *Reader's Digest*, January 1978, pp. 183–190.

Stopford, Francis. *The Romance of the Jewels*. Printed in London for private circulation, 1920.

Streeter, Edwin E. *The Great Diamonds of the World*. London: George Ben & Co., 1882.

Sultan Abdul Hamid II. *Catalogue de Bijoux*. Collection catalogue published in Paris, 1911.

Tavernier, Jean-Baptiste. *Travels in India*, Vols. 1 and 2. Translated by V. Bal. New York: Macmillan & Co., 1889.

"The Fabulous Killam Jewels." *Weekend*, No. 47, 1967, pp. 22–23.

"The Gem and the Curse." *Newsweek*, April 18, 1949.

"Those Diamond Blues, Music by Peggy Joyce." *The New York World*, March 13, 1928.

"$300,000 Diamond for Peggy Joyce—Buys It Herself." *New York Daily News*, March 13, 1928.

"$300,000 Gem Bought by Peggy Hopkins Joyce." *New York Herald Tribune*, March 13, 1928.

Tupper, Elsie and Harmon. "King of Diamonds." *Cosmopolitan*, April 1947, pp. 48–112.

Tupper, Elsie and Harmon. "Man with the Million Dollar Glitter." *Colliers Magazine*, May 21, 1949, pp. 63–66.

"25,000 Hindus Hail Miss Miller, Bride." *New York Times*, March 19, 1928.

Twining, Lord. *A History of the Crown Jewels of Europe*. London: Batsford Press, 1960.

Van Biljon, Madeleine. "Setting Pretty." *Fair Lady*, July 12, 1967, pp. 25–27.

Vever, Henri. *La Bijouterie Française au XIX Siècle*. Paris: H. Floury, 1908.

Weiden, Edward St. Clair. *A Year with the Gaekwar of Baroda*. London: Hutchinson & Co., 1912.

Whipple, Sidney B. "Jonker Diamond, Miracle of Beauty in the Rough." *Oakland (California) Tribune*, June 30, 1935.

Whipple, Sidney B. "World's Biggest Diamond Picked Up on African Farm." *Houston (Texas) Press*, June 21, 1955.

PROJECT DIRECTOR: ALICE S. KELLER

DESIGN: HENRY RATZ

PHOTOGRAPHY: HERBERT GILES (UNLESS OTHERWISE NOTED WITH THE PHOTO)

TYPOGRAPHY: THOMPSON TYPE, SAN DIEGO, CALIFORNIA

PRINTING: DAI NIPPON, JAPAN